Victor Ghoshe is an award-winning Indian author and international strategist whose work bridges literature, behavioural science, branding and social transformation. Ghoshe is best known for the *Eric Roy* historical adventure series—*The Job Charnock Riddle* and *Tomb of God*—both bestsellers, with *Tomb of God* topping WHSmith's Indian Writing charts for over six months earning him the Author of the Year (Fiction). Acclaimed by *The Times of India* as "our own Da Vinci Code" and described by *The Telegraph* as a cinematic, Lee Child–meets–Dan Brown thriller, his writing is distinguished by deep historical research, narrative intelligence and philosophical depth. *Tomb of God* is also listed among the United Kingdom's Best Literature selections for high-school reading.

Parallel to his literary career, Ghoshe is an internationally respected behavioural studies scholar and global strategist with over twenty-eight years of leadership in branding, communication, and social and behaviour change strategies. Trained at the BBC Academy, London, and Yale University, he has worked as senior adviser to BBC Media Action and creative head at DDB Mudra, shaping high-impact campaigns for global brands. His work in collaboration with governments and institutions including the Gates Foundation, UNDP and BBC has also influenced public policy and social transformation across South Asia and Sub-Saharan Africa.

A sought-after thinker on human behaviour, systems change and future readiness, Ghoshe's research papers on branding and behavioural design have been published in international journals, translated into multiple languages, and earned scholarships and recognition across continents.

He currently lectures on social and behaviour change and mass communication at the Indian Institute of Mass Communication, New Delhi.

Future Proof

Masterstrokes to Outthink and Outplay AI

VICTOR GHOSHE

First published in 2026 by

Om> EDGE An Imprint of **Om Books International**

Corporate & Editorial Office
A-12, Sector 64, Noida 201 301
Uttar Pradesh, India
Phone: +91 120 477 4100
Email: editorial@ombooks.com
Website: www.ombooksinternational.com

Sales Office
107, Ansari Road, Darya Ganj,
New Delhi 110 002, India
Phone: +91 11 4000 9000
Fax: +91 11 2327 8091
Email: sales@ombooks.com
Website: www.ombooks.com

ISBN: 978-93-6395-081-8

Printed in India

10 9 8 7 6 5 4 3 2 1

"*The world will not be inherited by the strongest, it will be inherited by those most able to change.*"

Charles Darwin

To

my parents, who taught me how to see the world;

my wife, Juthika, who pushes me beyond my creative limits;

my sons, Shivank and Hrishaant, who remind me every day to

remain curious, playful and human

Contents

INTRODUCTION

When the steam engine was invented, it did not just transform industry and commerce, it transformed lives. When the internet was born, it did not merely change communication, it redefined relationships, economies and power. And now, as artificial intelligence begins to reshape the world with the same, or perhaps even greater velocity, we find ourselves at yet another pivotal moment in human history.

Unlike past revolutions, AI is not waiting for us to respond. It is not politely knocking on the door of our industries; it is already inside, rewriting the rules, often faster than we can comprehend. For most people, the instinct is to either panic or freeze. But neither is helpful. What we need instead is preparation—not just technological, but emotional, cognitive and ethical.

The most consequential revolutions do not always arrive with fanfare. They seep into our lives. Quietly at first, like a new word whispered in a crowded room. And then, before we realize, they become the grammar of our world.

Artificial intelligence is one such revolution, and it is not coming, it is here. It is already in our conversations, our classrooms and our boardrooms. And now, increasingly, in our decisions.

We are living through a profound shift—not only in the tools we use but in the very *terms* by which we live, learn and lead. And yet, many of our systems—educational, political, societal, professional— are still oriented towards a past that no longer exists.

This book prepares us for what lies ahead. It is not about artificial intelligence. It is a book about human intelligence, human adaptability and, above all, human sense of responsibility.

I am not a computer scientist. I do not write algorithms or build neural networks. My world has been that of human behaviours and change—how individuals evolve under pressure, how institutions manage disruption and how entire communities re-imagine themselves in moments of existential challenge.

My colleagues around the world know me as a strategist and behavioural researcher who has spent years helping organizations ranging from Fortune 500 companies to international agencies, community level change-makers and government departments. With all those works and experiences I am approaching AI not as a technologist but as a translator between machine logic and human intuition and imagination.

I wrote this book because I strongly believe in the human potential to adapt and thrive. The question isn't whether AI will change our lives. It already is changing it. The real question is: Will we adapt in time to harness it?

This book discusses key challenges and pairs them with deeply human, future-forward solutions or masterstrokes. The solutions are based on my lifelong research on human behaviour, change, and the understanding of human-centred strategies and reflections on works of some of the world's most influential thinkers—Andrew Ng, Fei-Fei Li, Andrej Karpathy, Demis Hassabis, Geoffrey Hinton and Yuval Noah Harari.

These are practical, philosophical and urgent strategies.

For over two decades, I have worked across India, Bangladesh, Afghanistan, Ghana, Ethiopia, the Maldives and beyond, helping governments, global corporations and civil society networks shape change that is not just effective, but ethical and enduring. My deepest focus has been on using design thinking and human-centred design to build resilient communities and systems that can absorb shocks, recover rapidly and emerge wiser.

Whether it was building skills and rebuilding trust after natural disasters in coastal Sri Lanka and Maldives; co-creating change management campaign frameworks for Ethiopian and Ghanaian government; improving health-seeking behaviour in the villages of India or understanding gender issues in Afghanistan, the one lesson that echoed across geographies was that technology may catalyze change, but people metabolize it. The real question is not what AI can do; it is how we absorb and respond to that power.

Because this revolution, like every previous one, will eventually come down to human choices—who designs the systems; who interprets the outputs; who gets affected, included, excluded, monitored and empowered; and who bears the unintended consequences.

We are not dealing with a technological transition. We are dealing with a psychological, ethical and cultural transformation—one that demands a new kind of a mindset altogether.

The ones who will thrive in this era are not those who know the most about AI, but those who understand how it intersects with human life and how it alters motivation, behaviour, emotion, trust and social contracts. These are not peripheral concerns. They are the core of the new human intelligence.

This book is not a survival manual. It is a rehearsal space—a way for us to mentally, emotionally and ethically prepare for the storms that are already underway. Each chapter explores a tension at the heart of our new reality—emotional burnout in high-tech workplaces, the collapse of career identity in a world of automation, the loss of agency in systems optimized for efficiency and the loneliness beneath hyper-connectivity.

For each of these, I offer insights drawn not from code, but human code of curiosity, resilience, empathy, imagination and strategic foresight.

Each chapter decodes a specific threat or transformation. From job loss to data bias, from creative disruption to decision overload, and each challenge is paired with a human-centric response. These responses include:

- How to sharpen emotional intelligence in an era of machine logic
- How to develop multi-domain thinking
- Why narrative framing is your greatest professional asset
- How to build moral reasoning that keeps pace with technological change
- How to partner with AI as a co-creator, not a competitor

This book will not ask you to memorize technical terms. It will ask you to look in the mirror and ask yourself questions that machines cannot answer for you:

- How do I remain irreplaceable—not because of what I know, but because of *how* I think?
- How do I make decisions in systems I no longer fully understand?
- How do I practise ethics at the speed of innovation?
- How do I remain human—not despite the machine, but beside it?

In the field of design thinking, innovation is not about knowing all the answers it is about identifying and framing the right problems; in other words, writing the perfect "problem statements". This wisdom has never been more urgent because today, the danger is not just in what AI can do, but in what we forget to ask it not to do.

In my field of work, which is about social and behaviour change and designing human-centred interventions, I have seen the power of asking the right questions.

In short, this book is an invitation to develop ethical imagination—the capacity to see not just what is convenient, but what is just. To build a new kind of fluency—not with code, but with creative thinking. And to become the kind of person who can translate between data and meaning, between algorithms and ethics, and between information and wisdom.

Because in this new world, the most sought-after professionals will not be the ones with the highest IQ or the most advanced degrees. They will be the ones who ask better questions. The ones who sense when and where power is shifting, and know how to manage it responsibly.

Let me be clear, the challenge ahead is not merely technical, but civilizational. We are reshaping not just jobs, but worldviews. We are not just talking about economies, but relationships. And the cost of unchecked acceleration is not just error, it is harm. We need leaders who can pause; professionals who can reflect and citizens of the world who can imagine.

That is what this book is about. And I am just a translator between machine logic and human intuition. I wrote this book as a fellow traveller who has witnessed the chaos of change; someone who has sat in silence with communities rebuilding after loss; and someone who has spent years decoding the psychology of resistance and resilience. And who now sees that AI, for all its novelty, is a mirror held up to human nature rather than a disruption to it.

In this book I want to tell you about how to think, decide and express in ways that machines can't replicate. The insights are practical yet profound. You will find real-world cases, distilled analogies and action steps that do not require a tech background but demand a mindset shift. With my signature logic and lore method, I translate the wisdom of the most brilliant minds in the AI space into lessons for professionals, students, entrepreneurs, parents, house-makers and policymakers who want to ride the "AI wave".

If you are reading this, you are already sensing the shift. You know that waiting for certainty is no longer a strategy. That agility, not authority, is the new edge. And that insight, not fear, is the posture we need.

In the coming decade I see three possible scenarios emerging:

1. *The automator's paradise:* Artificial intelligence performs 80 per cent of white-collar tasks. Creativity becomes outsourced. Human boredom and burnout skyrocket.

2. *The hybrid mind:* Humans learn to work with AI in symbiotic ways. Society reorganizes around creative collaboration, learning and reinvention.

3. *The controlled collapse:* Poor governance, failure of ethics and economic inequality fuel instability. Artificial intelligence becomes a tool for misinformation, polarization and manipulation.

Which scenario prevails will depend not on machines but on humans.

In the end, AI is not about artificial intelligence. It is about *amplified* intelligence. And what it amplifies most is your character, your clarity and your curiosity.

Whether you are a management professional, a software engineer, a designer, a teacher, an entrepreneur or a young adult, this book will equip you with the essential mindset and tools to not only survive the AI wave but also become the most sought after professional because of it.

You don't need to become an AI expert. You need to become AI-compatible, and that is what this book will help you be.

Believe me, this book is not your shield but your compass.

Let us begin.

UNDERSTANDING THE IMAGINATION GAP

Why Some of Us Might Miss the AI Boat

How human short-sightedness and comfort zones prevent people from adapting to exponential tech shifts, and why foresight and imagination is the new survival skill.

On a sunny morning in 2023, Geoffrey Hinton, better known as the "Godfather of AI", walked away from Google, sounding an alarm louder than most of Silicon Valley dared to hear. The British-Canadian cognitive psychologist and computer scientist who had laid the foundation for deep learning warned that the very systems he helped create might soon surpass human control. He told the

BBC some of the dangers of AI chatbots were quite scary. "Right now, they are not more intelligent than us, as far as I can tell. But I think they soon may be." His concern wasn't a fringe worry; it was a wake-up call. But how many heard it?

Around the same time, academic and public intellectual Yuval Noah Harari cautioned that our collective inability to imagine what lies ahead might prove more dangerous than any machine. In his words, "History is being written faster than our ability to read it."

And yet, most professionals—engineers, marketers, educators, even tech executives—continue business as usual with emails, meetings, deadlines.

Why? Because the imagination gap blinds them.

Use more imagination, not data

It is not a lack of tools or talent that is keeping people behind; it is a lack of imagination. It is the comfort of routines and the illusion of control in a world changing faster than any generation before. We are not just missing the boat—we are building sandcastles while the tide of artificial intelligence reshapes the entire shoreline.

Look around, AI is not just evolving—it is accelerating. It is already drafting legal memos, diagnosing rare diseases, designing brand identities, writing code, composing music and teaching children to read. And yet, professionals still treat it as novelty—fun to play with, but not yet essential. What they don't see is that the revolution won't arrive with a press release. It is already unfolding in quiet, systemic shifts that will render entire skill-sets obsolete before job descriptions catch up.

There is something deeply human about underestimating exponential change. Our minds are built to predict linear progress. We assume tomorrow will be much like today, but with incremental improvements. That assumption worked for most of human history. But AI does not follow the rules of gradual change; it doubles in capability with each breakthrough. That is why yesterday's impossibility becomes today's prototype and tomorrow's expectation.

But awareness is not the same as readiness.

Most people acknowledge that AI is important. They have read a few articles, tried out a chatbot and maybe even added "prompt engineering" to their LinkedIn skills. But very few have stopped to fundamentally reconsider what their profession might look like in a world where cognitive tasks are no longer uniquely human. And even fewer have asked themselves, *What role do I play in a world where machines can think?*

That is the imagination gap, and it is not about intelligence; it is about mental models. Many people are simply solving old problems with new tools, without realizing that entirely new problems and opportunities now exist. They use AI to draft faster emails, but not to rethink how communication itself could be redesigned. They automate tedious tasks, but fail to question whether those tasks should exist at all.

This is not a critique of individuals; it is a critique of systems. Our education trains us to become efficient within existing paradigms, not to question the paradigms themselves. Most workplaces reward predictability and deliverables, not radical curiosity. And our culture valorizes productivity over perspective. In such an environment, imagination becomes a liability—something to indulge in your free time, not something to bring to the quarterly meeting.

In the age of AI, imagination becomes the last competitive advantage. Isn't that ironic?

"Logic will get you from A to B. Imagination will take you everywhere."

—Albert Einstein

Machines can analyze, compute, generate and simulate, but they cannot dream in the way humans can. They cannot imagine a world that has never existed and then take steps to build it. That remains our domain. But only if we choose to use it.

The question is not whether AI will replace jobs because it will. The questions that we need to ask ourselves are:

- Who will invent the new ones?
- Who will reframe industries?
- Who will challenge outdated assumptions and design new ways to teach, heal, build and connect?

The answers won't be found in a résumé. It will be found in a mindset.

History is full of moments where technology reshaped what it meant to be human, for example, the printing press, the steam engine, electricity, the internet. In each case, there were those who saw the future early—not because they had more data, but because they had more imagination.

Artificial intelligence is not the enemy of work, but it is the enemy of complacency. Those waiting for the "AI moment" to arrive may already be too late. The moment has passed. We are now living in the aftermath of its arrival.

So the real danger isn't being left behind by the machine. It is being left behind by those who dared to imagine what the machine makes possible.

Stop staring at the shore. Turn your eyes towards the open sea. The boats are leaving. Will you still be on the beach, holding a clipboard? Or will you learn to sail in uncharted waters?

We need to ask the uncomfortable questions

Throughout history, the inability to foresee technological disruption has not been rooted in ignorance, but in a fundamental limitation of human imagination. The horse-drawn carriage industry, despite its centuries of accumulated wisdom, failed to anticipate the advent of the automobile. Similarly, the photography giants, with all their technical mastery, did not predict that the smartphone would make everyone a photographer and archivist. Perhaps most poignantly, Encyclopedia Britannica, the very symbol of curated human knowledge, was blindsided by Wikipedia—a decentralized, freely editable platform fuelled by millions of anonymous contributors. These were not isolated failures; they were systemic blind spots. They reveal how deeply humans cling to models of the world that have served them in the past, mistakenly assuming that tomorrow will merely be an improved version of today.

This cognitive trap, known as "status quo bias", persists across all professions. A finance executive who trusts that traditional spreadsheets will forever underpin corporate decision-making fails to see the rise of autonomous AI-driven financial analytics. A legal practitioner, immersed in case law and human argumentation, underestimates the speed at which AI can parse precedents, predict outcomes and assist judges. Educators, often heralded as agents of change, can themselves become anchored to familiar pedagogies, unable to envision a world where individualized AI tutors offer hyper-personalized education to every student. Each example illustrates a dangerous presumption that change will come gently, on human terms, and only after ample warning.

Yet the nature of technological progress, particularly in the world of AI, defies linear expectations. Artificial intelligence operates on an exponential curve. In its early stages, this curve appears deceptively slow, fostering complacency. Early developments seem trivial: a chatbot here, an image generator there. But the curve bends sharply upwards. Innovations build upon one another, compounding capabilities at an accelerating rate. What appears laughable today can render entire industries obsolete tomorrow. This is why early warnings are so easily dismissed as noise until they coalesce into irreversible transformations.

Compounding this problem are organizational cultures that prize short-term predictability over long-term vision. Corporations reward managers for delivering quarterly results, optimizing existing processes and minimizing risks. Little space exists for cultivating disruptive thinking. Strategic planning sessions focus on incremental improvements rather than asking uncomfortable questions like "What if our most profitable service becomes free tomorrow?" or "What if an AI tool renders 80 per cent of our workforce redundant?" In the absence of such questioning, institutions drift unknowingly towards the edge of disruption.

Beneath these structural and cognitive barriers lies a deeper psychological truth: change is terrifying. The fear of obsolescence haunts professionals more profoundly than they admit. To question the durability of one's skills, to imagine a world where accumulated expertise loses value, provokes existential anxiety. As a coping mechanism, individuals, and even organizations and governments, rationalize the status quo, clinging to familiar patterns and dismissing emerging threats.

Ultimately, the failure to see what is coming is not a failure of information. It is a failure of "imagination courage" (a deliberate coinage, not a formally established term in psychology or behavioural science literature), which I believe is the human ability to face an unfamiliar future and still choose to move towards it. In a rapidly evolving world, survival will belong to those who dare to question their most cherished assumptions, and to envision realities fundamentally different from the one they inhabit today.

How not to become a character in a machine's script

Hinton's resignation from Google did not merely mark the end of an illustrious career; it marked a historical pivot point in humanity's relationship with artificial intelligence. The Godfather of AI spent decades building the very foundations of deep learning, the technology now driving today's AI revolution. Yet in stepping away, he publicly acknowledged an unsettling truth that AI systems have grown so complex that even their creators no longer fully understand them. These are no longer passive tools awaiting human commands; they are statistical black boxes capable of making decisions that increasingly affect human lives in hiring, policing, warfare, healthcare without transparent reasoning. In Hinton's warnings, a subtle but profound shift emerges: a builder's optimism gives way to the steward's dread.

Harari frames the stakes from a civilizational and narrative perspective. According to him, humanity's unique strength lies not in muscle or speed, but in its ability to believe in shared narratives—nations, corporations, laws and currencies—all constructed myths sustained by collective belief. The human race has built empires, religions, markets and civilizations through these narratives. The power to imagine and propagate stories shaped the destiny of humankind.

But the rise of AI threatens to short-circuit this evolutionary advantage. As machines learn not only to process language but to generate persuasive, emotionally resonant narratives, they begin to rival humans in the art of storytelling. When AI can simulate empathy more consistently than a human, when it can craft political speeches, advertising campaigns, or even religious sermons with tailored emotional precision, humans risk losing control over the stories that define their reality. In such a world, truth becomes harder to distinguish from manipulation; authenticity gives way to algorithmic influence. Narrative sovereignty—the ability to author and own the human story—begins to slip away.

Hinton's anxiety and Harari's concern reveal a deeper crisis: humanity is creating cognitive tools whose capabilities outstrip its ethical frameworks. As engineers race to make systems smarter, ethicists, legislators and philosophers lag behind. Humanity possesses no equivalent "deep learning" model for meaning, governance or restraint. As a result, society accelerates into a future laden with intelligence but devoid of wisdom.

Without systemic checks, the danger is twofold. First, AI systems could amplify existing inequalities, biases and power imbalances, cloaked behind the facade of technological neutrality.

Second, by assuming narrative control, AI could shape desires, choices and values at scales and speeds no human institution could match. The manipulation of collective imagination would no longer be a tool reserved for demagogues or advertisers; it would become industrialized, automated and invisible.

Therefore, Hinton's resignation and Harari's warnings should not be seen as isolated alarms, but as parts of a single urgent message: humanity must not only innovate faster, but also imagine deeper. Ethical foresight must become as sophisticated as technological engineering. Otherwise, the species that once ruled the world through storytelling may find itself out-narrated by its own creations, becoming a character in someone, or something, else's script.

Who will thrive in this new world?

It won't be the person who has mastered every tool. It will be the one who has mastered how to think. The new professional must combine logic with vision and competence with conscience.

You don't need to be a coder, but you need to understand how AI shifts the nature of choice. You don't need to be a philosopher, but you must grasp that every technological act is a moral one.

In a world reshaped by AI, the most prized skills will be:

- *Systems thinking*—seeing beyond individual tools to entire ecosystems.
- *Ethical reasoning*—asking not only "Can we?" but "Should we?"
- *Narrative foresight*—imagining alternate futures and preparing for them.

- *Emotional intelligence*—building trust in a landscape saturated with simulation.
- *Curiosity*—the capacity to stay a student forever.

The best professionals will be those who create bridges across different disciplines, between humans and machines, and between what is and what could be.

This is an urgent call, not a wish list. Just as the industrial era demanded literacy, the AI era demands visionary literacy. Not everyone will answer. But those who do will shape not just careers, but civilizations.

Shaping the future, staying futureproof

We are not merely facing a technological deficit in the twenty-first century; we are grappling with a crisis of narrative. The stories that dominate our media are polarized, swinging between utopia and dystopia. On the one hand, we are promised a future of boundless possibility, where AI liberates humanity from mundane tasks and enriches our lives. On the other, we are warned of a looming dystopia, where machines rise to dominate us, leaving millions unemployed and our personal freedoms compromised. Both extremes may have some grain of truth, but neither captures the full complexity of the technological landscape we find ourselves in.

Policymakers are equally reactive, often responding to crises as they unfold rather than anticipating them. Their focus tends to be on managing immediate risks rather than envisioning and preparing for long-term societal shifts. Universities and educational institutions focus heavily on teaching students how to write code but neglect to instil an understanding of techno-ethics or the human implications of automation. In business, many leaders are fixated on quarterly profits, driven by short-term goals that disregard the long-term consequences of their decisions. The result is a world that rushes towards innovation without foresight and consideration needed to guide it responsibly.

In this environment, where the pace of AI evolution outstrips our ability to understand and manage it, this narrow vision becomes perilous. Why do so many still miss the AI boat? Because they believe they are still anchored in the harbour, thinking they have time to react. In reality, the tide is already pulling them out to sea.

What is required in this moment of uncertainty is what the Marxist philosopher Ernst Bloch referred to as "concrete hope". This is not a vague fantasy or naive escapism, but a grounded, actionable form of imagination. It is the belief that the future is not a predetermined force we must passively accept but something that can be shaped–if we dare to shape it. Concrete hope demands that we ask radical questions that are too often ignored or sidestepped in the rush towards innovation and profit. Questions like:

- What kind of future do we want to build?
- What do we owe to future generations in terms of fairness, sustainability and ethics?
- How do we ensure that ethics and human values are embedded at the speed of technological innovation, so that we are not left with systems that undermine the very principles we hold dear?

If we fail to ask these questions, we will drift aimlessly at the mercy of forces beyond our control. But with these questions in mind, we can lead by proactively shaping the future rather than merely reacting to its consequences.

How to reclaim the human advantage

As machine intelligence grows sharper, faster and more autonomous, a quiet anxiety begins to thread itself through all lives. Across industries, from law firms to classrooms, from hospitals to newsrooms, the fear is palpable:

- Will we still be needed?
- Will AI render us obsolete?

Such fears are not entirely unfounded because machines are outpacing humans in a wide range of cognitive tasks. They translate languages in milliseconds, detect anomalies in medical scans, write functional code, and even compose music and poetry. *Echoes of the Universe* is a poetry collection by Dawson Hunt and ChatGPT. The *Aum Golly* series is a fascinating experiment in AI-generated poetry. Some have even written novels. *The Day A Computer Writes A Novel* is a groundbreaking book from Japan. It was written by an AI program developed by the Sato-Matsuzaki Laboratory. But the error lies in mistaking computation for consciousness and optimization for meaning.

The human advantage was never solely in speed or precision. It has always rested on a deeper, more elusive quality, which is the capacity to assign significance where none objectively exists. A mathematical formula has logic, but it does not have grief. A poem has structure, but also sorrow. Meaning is a function of presence, of attention, of memory and of moral depth.

In every civilization, the true power of humans has been their ability to translate existence into purpose. While AI may outperform in patterns, predictions and probabilities, it cannot form intentions. It cannot hold ethical dilemmas, or mourn a loss, or redefine its life through a brushstroke or a prayer. Machines can predict the weather, but they cannot appreciate the sound of thunder or the smell of wet soil after rain. *Not yet.*

In this emerging reality, the human role is refined, not diminished. Professionals who centre their work in empathy, in ethics, in cultural imagination, will not be replaced—they will become indispensable. The capacity to understand a patient's unspoken fear, to design a public service that respects not only data but dignity, to craft policies that consider not just efficiency but equity are not tasks that can be uploaded. Artificial intelligence may become the world's most powerful assistant, but humanity must remain the world's most powerful meaning-maker.

Machines can play chess, compose symphonies and answer emails, but they cannot fall in love; they cannot forgive; they cannot dream with purpose.

What makes us human?

It is not our processing power but our capacity for meaning—the uniquely human act of turning experience into insight, emotion into intention and existence into purpose. It is our capacity through which we make sense of the world and choose who we become in that world.

Meaning is not data; it is the fire behind art, the soul of community and the core of ethics. In the age of AI, these will be differentiators, not luxuries.

Professionals who build meaning into their work whether through leadership, design, education or policy will thrive. Those who merely execute tasks will compete with systems that don't sleep.

We don't need to compete with AI. We need to complete it.

Let AI handle repetition, calculation, optimization. Let humans handle love, wisdom, vision. That is not a romantic fantasy; it is a design principle.

Rather than competing with machines on the terrain they dominate, the wise move is to reposition. Let algorithms process and let humans interpret. Let systems predict and let societies choose. Let machines manage complexity and humans nurture conscience.

This shift is not a rejection of technology; it is a design imperative. The human–machine collaboration must be built on complementarity. The future professional will be measured not by how efficiently they imitate AI, but by how efficiently they enhance it through perspective, ethics and vision.

The path forward lies not in resisting technology, but in remembering humanity. The greatest loss would not be losing to AI, but losing the essence of what it means to be human while trying to keep pace.

The imagination advantage

The power of imagination has long been celebrated in the arts, tolerated in marketing, but often dismissed as impractical in more "serious" domains. Yet history reveals a different truth: every leap in civilization, every societal pivot, every scientific revolution has been born from the ability to imagine what did not exist.

Imagination is not a luxury; it is a discipline. It is not the realm of dreamers detached from reality; it is the training ground of visionaries who shape it.

In the age of AI, where machines increasingly dominate the territory of logic, analysis and efficiency, imagination is no longer just a creative add-on. It is a strategic necessity. The imagination gap—the inability to conceive of alternative futures—will prove far more dangerous than any skill gap.

Imagination must now be practised deliberately, even methodically. Professionals must treat it as seriously as they treat metrics and forecasts. Scenario planning should no longer be confined to corporate boardrooms or government agencies—it should be a regular exercise for individuals, teams and communities alike.

Imagination is not a trait; it is a discipline. Just like physical fitness, it must be trained.

The questions worth asking are no longer limited to "What is?" but must stretch to "What *if*?" and "What *else*?"

- What if the very service one offers is automated tomorrow?
- What if a core assumption behind one's industry collapses?
- What if a new intelligence begins to define what is valuable?

So, what is the way forward?

Set aside an hour each week to read science fiction—not as escape, but as foresight. Science fiction has been predicting AI since 1816 when Mary Shelley's *Frankenstein* warned us of the dangers of creating artificial beings. Engage with people outside your field, learn about their works, understand how they plan to cope with the changes that AI is bringing in their fields. Ask your team, "What would we do if our core service became automated tomorrow?"

Create future scenarios. Map unintended consequences. Study history to not just to admire progress, but to see its fragile roots.

Treat imagination not as indulgence, but as strategy.

As decision-makers in tomorrow's world, the imagination gap is our greatest threat and our greatest opportunity.

Through such exercises, individuals begin to reframe their relationship with—not as something to be feared, but as something to be anticipated and shaped. When teams from different disciplines and social backgrounds come together to explore wild, uncomfortable and unlikely futures, they begin to build resilience. They begin to design new ethical maps and social strategies not based on past data alone, but on the audacity to ask different questions.

Imagination is not only forward-looking, it is backward-reaching too. It understands that every present norm was once a radical deviation. The rights of children, the abolition of slavery and the idea of global human rights emerged from someone's refusal to accept the world as it was. They were, in their time, acts of civil imagination.

Thus, the future will not belong to the most knowledgeable, but to the most imaginative. Those who can look beyond existing systems, invent new frameworks and make sense of chaos will shape what comes next. While AI writes stories or paint images, it cannot conceive of futures it has not been trained on. Humans, uniquely, can.

As AI narrows its path to what is statistically likely, human intelligence must widen its gaze to what is ethically desirable and socially sustainable. In doing so, the act of imagination is reclaimed— not as fantasy, but as foresight. Not as escapism, but as evolution.

In a world rushing towards automation, imagination may well become the final frontier of human agency.

How I learned it

Finally, we understand an empowering truth: the AI era will not be defined by machines alone, but by how humans choose to use them. And those who develop the imagination to see past the present will be the ones steering the ship and not watching it sail away. Now, let me tell you about something relevant that I have experienced and learned.

Looking back, the first time I truly understood the destructive power of cognitive inertia was not through academic research or global case studies, but during my work with the Government of Bihar to improve public health outcomes. We entered the state with technical competence, tested behaviour-change models and the confidence that global best practices would naturally take root. Yet, for months, nothing changed—not the behaviours, not the indicators, not the outcomes. On paper, we were doing everything "right," but on the ground, we were failing. And it was not a failure of strategy; it was a failure of imagination. We were unable, in those early months, to see Bihar as Bihar saw itself.

I remember realizing, with uncomfortable clarity, that we were not failing because communities did not understand the need for better family health; we were failing because we did not understand their world. Health was not their first priority—survival was; prosperity was; a sense of dignity was. The global behaviour-change theories we trusted had never imagined a reality where daily existence was so precarious that vaccination reminders meant little against hunger, debt and uncertainty. The psychological inertia wasn't theirs alone; it was ours. We were holding on to familiar frameworks, established roles and inherited worldviews. We wanted communities to change without changing the stories we told about them.

This realization emerged slowly, almost painfully, until one day, in a moment of absolute professional desperation, the idea came: *Swasthya Bihar, Samriddh Bihar*—a major state-specific behaviour change campaign; a simple but radical reframing of the problem.

What if we stopped talking about "improving health" as an isolated goal? What if we spoke instead about prosperity, growth, possibility and placed improved health as the foundation on which that future could stand? It was a philosophical shift as much as a communication shift. A new narrative, one that communities could adopt without feeling judged, lectured, or left out. It was, in essence, an invitation to imagine a better life. And imagination, once unlocked, turned resistance into momentum.

The campaign went on to become the largest public health communication initiative in India, reaching all thirty-eight districts and contributing to a remarkable decline in Bihar's infant mortality rate from forty-four deaths per 1,000 live births in 2011 to twenty-seven by 2020 (As per *Sample Registration System (SRS) Statistical Report, 2020.* Published on 22 September 2022.) Those numbers carry the weight of countless stories, but for me, they also carry a quiet lesson: no technical intervention succeeds unless the human mind is ready to see a different future. Change does not begin with information; it begins with imagination. And imagination, when blocked, can jeopardize the best of the strategies.

As I write about AI today, I realize the pattern is exactly the same. Professionals are not unprepared because technology is too advanced; they are unprepared because their imagination is too narrow. We cling to old roles, old assumptions, old definitions of intelligence and relevance. My years in Bihar taught me that the greatest threat to progress is not the lack of knowledge but the refusal to re-imagine what we think we already know. The AI era will not reward the most technical minds, but will reward the most adaptable ones—those who can step out of inherited worldviews and see the world not as it was, but as it is becoming. That is how

we futureproof ourselves. And that is how we stay human in the age
of intelligent machines.

GROW TOGETHER NOT APART WITH ARTIFICIAL INTELLIGENCE

Mastering Meta-Learning

How our brains evolved and helped us survive through ages, and it is time to evolve again.

In 2017, Andrew Ng the co-founder of Google Brain and Coursera, and one of the most influential voices in artificial intelligence, famously declared, "AI is the new electricity." It was a bold analogy. Just as electricity transformed every industry, from manufacturing to healthcare, AI, he said, would redefine how value is created in the twenty-first century. It was a statement that energized boardrooms, think tanks and technologists across the world.

But behind this headline-making statement lies a quieter, perhaps even more transformative idea: lifelong learning is a survival skill. Ng often emphasizes that in the AI-powered future, static expertise is a liability. The edge lies with those who can learn, unlearn and relearn on demand, at speed and in context.

Around the same time, Andrej Karpathy—then director of AI at Tesla—was developing another foundational concept: Software 2.0. In this paradigm, we move beyond traditional programming where humans write explicit rules. Instead, machines learn from examples. Neural networks replace hand-coded logic. The new "coder" is a data curator, and the true power lies in shaping the training environment. It is not what the machine is told to do—it is what it learns to do, based on the signals it is fed.

Ng and Karpathy come from different vantage points but their insights converge on a single, inescapable truth: the future belongs not to those who know the most, but to those who learn the fastest. Not just humans but machines as well. And it is here that we must pause and reassess what we mean by learning in the age of acceleration.

For humans, learning has traditionally been linear and hierarchical. We start with facts, build to principles and eventually develop expertise. For machines, learning is pattern recognition at scale, unconstrained by time, fatigue or bias at least in the traditional human sense. And yet, as machines grow in their learning capacity, the nature of human learning becomes even more vital—not less.

Why?

Because the smarter the machines become, the more important human values become. A machine can optimize for outcomes but only a human can truly define what is better. A system can learn to recommend, rank or route but only a human can question whether the problem it is solving is worth solving at all.

This is the paradox of progress: as AI becomes more autonomous, human intentionality becomes more critical.

To navigate this paradox, we need a new model—a loop, not a ladder. Traditional models of learning are built around ascent: get the degree, climb the career, reach the top. But success in the AI age is more about momentum than mastery. We are shifting from a world of knowledge economies to one of learning economies. In this new economy, the learning loop is the ultimate engine.

The learning loop is continuous, flexible and cross-disciplinary. It involves sensing, interpreting, experimenting and iterating. Think of it as the heartbeat of adaptive intelligence—something both humans and machines can develop, but in profoundly different ways.

Machines learn through data feedback loops. Every click, correction or reinforcement helps refine the model. But humans learn through meaning feedback loops. We don't just take in information; we attach relevance, values and emotions. That is why co-evolution between humans and machines is not just technical—it is philosophical. It is not just about how fast the loop spins; it is about whether it spins in the right direction.

Today, many organizations are investing in machine learning infrastructure without investing in human learning infrastructure. That is like building race cars without training drivers. The result? Misalignment; mistrust; misuse. Machines optimize without understanding. Humans delegate without discernment.

If AI is to enhance our society rather than fragment it, we need to design symbiotic learning environments. Spaces where humans and machines learn together with each helping the other refine, calibrate and grow.

For professionals, this means shifting focus from acquiring skills to cultivating learning agility. It is not enough to know how to use AI tools. One must also know how to frame the right problems, ask the right questions and reflect on unintended consequences. The most advanced AI systems still need context, which is still a uniquely human gift.

For leaders, it means rethinking how talent is nurtured and how decisions are made. Learning ecosystems must be built into the DNA of teams as a core strategy, not as an afterthought. This includes not just upskilling workers, but also re-skilling the culture—rewarding curiosity, experimentation, and critical reflection over mere compliance and productivity.

And for society at large, it means confronting hard questions: What should machines never be allowed to learn? What kinds of decisions should never be delegated to algorithms? How do we ensure that human learning keeps pace not only in terms of speed, but also in terms of depth and ethics?

The age of acceleration demands more than innovation. It demands intentional, aligned and continuously evolving learning loops. It is not a race against machines. It is a race with ourselves to stay human in how we think, act and evolve.

The challenge is not that machines are learning too fast. It is that we might be learning too slowly, not in acquiring knowledge, but in adapting our mindset to a world where intelligence is no longer uniquely human.

This chapter is your compass to reorient your learning, or risk being outpaced not just by machines but by your own outdated assumptions.

Evolve with AI in the learning loop

The learning loop is about cause and consequence, and action and adaptation. You act. The world responds. You pause to reflect, make sense of the response and try again—refined, recalibrated. This is how infants learn to walk, how scientists develop hypotheses and how athletes improve their form. It is also how software learns to play chess, detect cancer or write code.

In both humans and machines, learning requires feedback. But while humans draw on stories, mentors, memories and emotions, machines rely on datasets, optimization functions and back-propagation. The machinery may be different, but the goal is the same: improve over time through response and correction. The human learning loop is deeply personal. It is shaped by fear, ego, trauma, culture and joy. It moves in fits and starts. Sometimes slow. Sometimes breakthrough-fast. It is non-linear and emotionally charged. One harsh comment from a teacher can cause a student to lose interest for years. One unexpected success can inspire a lifetime of exploration.

In contrast, machines don't feel shame. They don't get distracted. They don't need coffee or sleep. Their learning loops are structured, scalable and almost mechanical in their precision. They consume millions of examples and optimize continuously, often learning more in a day than a person could in a year. But this speed comes with a cost. They don't understand context. They don't question intention. And crucially, they don't know what *matters*—not yet.

This is where the synergy becomes spectacular. Imagine a loop where humans provide intention, creativity and context, while machines offer scale, memory and pattern recognition. The result is more than cooperation; it is co-evolution.

For instance, a doctor may observe a pattern in rare patient cases. An AI might detect a similar pattern across ten million patient records. The learning loop tightens. The doctor learns something new. The AI gets a better model. Both improve.

Or consider the design process. A human designer generates a prototype. The AI simulates user reactions, suggests changes and helps refine the model. The designer then interprets these insights not just for usability, but for emotional resonance. The loop becomes richer with each turn.

The most powerful learning loops today are not entirely human or entirely machine. They are hybrid. They are formed at the interface of biological wisdom and computational power.

However, this hybrid loop doesn't just happen. It must be designed. It must be made conscious.

That means asking:
- Where does human intuition still lead?
- Where can machines correct our blind spots?
- How do we close the loop quickly and ethically?
- Who gets to control the feedback?

Make no mistake: whoever shapes the feedback, shapes the learning.

This feedback loop has implications far beyond education. It affects how we build systems of justice, how we create equitable economies, how we treat the planet. A biased loop can reinforce inequality. A transparent loop can enhance empathy.

Therefore, AI versus humans is not the frontier. It is AI and humans working together in a loop where each side is evolving rather than just responding.

To participate in this loop consciously is not just to stay relevant, it is to stay human. In an age where machines are learning faster than ever, the question is not whether we can keep up. It is whether we can collaborate without losing ourselves.

Learning as a survival skill

For much of the twentieth century, education followed a predictable arc. You studied, graduated and got a job. Learning was front-loaded. It had a beginning, middle and an end. The assumption was simple: master a skill, apply it for thirty years and then retire.

That world is gone.

Today, knowledge is perishable. Textbooks don't change as quickly as technologies do. Entire industries are born, rise and die in the span of a single career. A job title that did not exist five years ago like "prompt engineer" or "AI ethics officer" can now fetch six-figure salaries. Static learning is a liability in this world.

Learning has become the new literacy. Not in the traditional sense of reading and writing but in the deeper sense of adapting, unlearning and relearning at speed. If the twentieth century prized experts, the twenty-first century rewards adaptive learners who can learn anything at any time and apply it across contexts.

This shift reframes education not as an event, but as a system. Not as something we consume, but something we design. The best learners today don't wait for permission. They create their own learning ecosystems by curating mentors, feedback, algorithms, routines and even digital tools that evolve with them.

This is what it means to become a learning architect. It is less about storing information and more about shaping environments that make learning inevitable. The most successful people in this era are not the ones with the highest IQ; they are the ones who build the strongest feedback loops.

Karpathy's Software 2.0 isn't just a technological idea; it is a cultural one. The old rule-based thinking where people memorized facts and followed procedures is being replaced by pattern-based thinking. We now operate in systems that learn, adapt and rewrite themselves continuously. And we must learn like that system if we want to thrive in it.

So what does adaptive learning look like in practice?

It looks like a product manager who tests five prototypes in a day using AI simulations and learns from each one. It looks like a teacher who co-creates lesson plans with chatbots and adjusts in real-time based on student responses. It looks like a policymaker who uses predictive analytics not just for efficiency but to identify unseen human needs.

It also looks like personal reinvention where a mid-career executive learns Python not to become a coder, but to think computationally; a parent reads behavioural science to better understand their child; and a retiree launches a podcast, learns video editing to master digital storytelling. This is not about becoming machines. It is about staying human *at speed*.

But learning at speed requires humility. It requires courage to admit what we don't know. It demands psychological safety to fail, reflect and restart without shame.

More importantly, it requires tools. AI can be that tool. Used well, it becomes a mirror for our blind spots, a tutor for our curiosity and a coach for our ambitions.

The learners of the future are not the ones with perfect answers; they are the ones with better questions, faster feedback and relentless curiosity.

In a world where stability is illusion, learning is the only real security. Thus, it is no longer optional; it is survival.

Don't be a passive consumer of machine output

Machines are no longer just tools, they have become collaborators and co-pilots in our thinking processes, companions in decision-making and even provocateurs of our imagination.

Consider the AI tutor that adapts its teaching style to each learner's pace, comprehension level and learning gaps. It does not just present information; it responds to your confusion, recalibrates the lesson and then tries again. It remembers what you struggled with last week and builds today's challenge around it. This isn't one-size-fits-all education. It is personalized learning scaled by code.

Or take large language models (LLMs). These systems don't simply retrieve information; they simulate dialogue, generate hypotheses and suggest multiple ways to express an idea. A writer can brainstorm headlines with an LLM. A lawyer can test counter-arguments. A designer can generate variations of a brief. Machines are increasingly becoming mirrors of our cognition with extensions into realms we may not have thought to explore alone.

Then there is reinforcement learning which involves algorithms that simulate thousands of possibilities in minutes. Whether it is optimizing supply chains, testing medical hypotheses or mastering complex decision environments, these agents can test what a human couldn't test in a lifetime.

What does all this mean for the human learner?

It means the way we learn must evolve not just to use machines, but to learn with them. Every interaction with a machine becomes an opportunity to refine your own cognition. When you ask a question to an AI, reflect on not just the answer, but on how the model reasoned or failed to reason. If it gives a biased answer, trace where that came from. If it produces creative output, try to reverse-engineer its structure. You are not just getting output; you are getting insight into an alternate type of intelligence.

In this dynamic, users are no longer passive consumers of machine output. They become co-educators. The questions we ask, the feedback we give, the examples we offer train the model. The better our questions, the better the machine becomes. The better the machine becomes, the more it challenges us to think differently, more deeply and more clearly.

This virtuous cycle where we train machines and machines train us is the new frontier of human development. It is not just about faster answers; it is about cultivating sharper minds. In learning from machines, we begin to learn more about our assumptions, our shortcuts, our creativity and our capacity to grow.

Teach machines to learn responsibly

While machines can learn fast, they do not know what to value. They optimize for objectives. If the objectives are poorly defined, biased or dangerous, the machine will learn the wrong lesson at scale.

This is where human learning reasserts its primacy because ethical reasoning, empathy and contextual awareness cannot be outsourced.

Just as parents shape a child's moral development, professionals must shape a machine's learning environment, which includes:

- curating diverse and representative datasets;
- auditing for unintended consequences;
- designing feedback loops that reinforce societal good, not just efficiency; and
- ensuring explainability, not just accuracy.

If human intelligence is the compass, machine intelligence is the accelerator. Without the former, the latter drives us blind.

Be a meta-learner

Meta-learning, or "learning to learn", is the next frontier. For us, this means understanding how we acquire skills, where our biases lie and how to self-correct.

For machines, it means building systems that can generalize learning strategies across tasks.

The convergence is clear:

- Humans must become more algorithmic in tracking their progress, testing hypotheses and iterating.
- Machines must become more human in understanding ambiguity, context and intent.

The new professional is not just a subject expert. They are a meta-learner. Someone who builds systems to continuously update themselves and others.

Practical steps to join the loop

Joining the learning loop does not require a PhD in artificial intelligence. It requires a mindset shift and deliberate practice.

Start with these steps:

- *Micro-learning rituals*: Dedicate 15 minutes a day to learn something adjacent to your field, using AI summaries (smart note-takers that instantly distil long information down to the key points) or simulations (digital sandboxes help testing real-world scenarios and predicting future outcomes without risk).

- *AI pair practice*: Use a chatbot or LLM as a brainstorming partner. Practise reframing problems. Explore alternative viewpoints. The table below gives an overview. It synthesizes the dominant AI platforms currently in use and the kinds of practice each supports. Rather than ranking tools, it maps their functional strengths to learning intent.

Platform/ Model	Access Type	Best For Practice
ChatGPT (OpenAI)	Free/Paid Subscription	General-purpose use, creative writing and understanding prompt dynamics.
Gemini (Google)	Free/Paid Subscription	Multimodal tasks (text/ image), coding and complex reasoning.
Claude (Anthropic)	Free/Paid Subscription	Excellent for handling very long documents and maintaining a specific tone.

Platform/Model	Access Type	Best For Practice
Perplexity AI	Free/Paid Subscription	Practise research and citation—it shows sources for its answers, which is great for validating information.
Notion AI / Microsoft Copilot	Free/Paid (Integrated)	Practise workflow integration—using AI to summarize notes, draft emails or generate project plans.

Created by the author

- *Reflective loops*: After using an AI tool (from above list), jot down what you learned about your own thought process. What assumptions did the tool challenge?

- *Reverse teaching*: Try teaching a concept back to the machine (AI), e.g., through prompting or fine-tuning. This deepens your grasp.

- *Design feedback systems*: Create dashboards or trackers for your personal learning goals. Treat your growth like a software update.

- *Cross-training*: Collaborate with people outside your domain using AI as a common ground. Watch how others learn.

How to align learning with human values

Acceleration is not new to humanity. Every era has had its momentum—from the printing press to the internet. But what is different about this moment is the scale and opacity of acceleration. Machines now learn faster than we do, act faster than we can respond and evolve faster than our systems are prepared to manage.

This acceleration without thoughtful alignment leads not to progress, but to chaos. Or worse—misaligned progress, where systems optimize for speed over values, for outcomes over understanding.

So, what does alignment look like in a world of accelerating intelligence?

It is not just about setting ethical guardrails. Alignment means synchronizing machine learning with human intention. It means ensuring that AI systems don't just optimize for metrics, but for meaning. It is less about hard constraints and more about soft stewardship, which involves embedding in machines a reflection of the world we want, not just the world that is.

To achieve this, we need shared language between disciplines. Engineers must speak to ethicists. Data scientists must learn from teachers. Psychologists must assist AI comprehend context and nuance. Shared values don't emerge from silos; they are constructed through dialogue and mutual learning.

Alignment also requires shared feedback loops. Think of it this way: when a diagnostic AI updates its model based on hospital data, that update does not exist in isolation. It alters how a doctor interacts with it. That interaction then changes future data collection. And so the loop continues.

This is why every act of learning—human or machine—is now a design decision. The way we teach machines to see the world ends up teaching us how we relate to that world. If AI learns from biased data, it amplifies those biases. If we feed it curiosity and compassion, it can reflect those back to us. We must be intentional. Let me explain this: We need to specify the desired human trait (like curiosity or empathy) in our input to prompt the AI to reflect it in its output.

Example of intentional input:

- Prompt (Curiosity): Research the history of telescopes, but focus on the key unanswered questions that still drive astronomers today.
- Result (Reflection): The AI provides a report that not only lists facts but also frames them in the context of persistent mysteries and future inquiry.

In this new era, alignment is not a technical challenge; it is a cultural one. It is about choosing what kind of intelligence we want to amplify. Let us not confuse acceleration for advancement. Let us ensure that in going faster; we are also going together towards something we consciously choose.

How I learned it

My first real encounter with meta-learning did not begin in a classroom or through any structured pedagogy. It began in the noisy, combustible, relentlessly demanding world of Indian advertising in the mid-1990s—a world that became my first laboratory of "learning how to learn". After studying communication design, I entered advertising as an art director. I believed I had chosen my path: visuals, layouts, typography. But very soon, I realized that in most agencies of that era, the copywriter was the hero—the one who owned the room, shaped the creative concept, voiced the idea, commanded the spotlight and finally walk up to the creative director's seat. Something in me responded to that imbalance not with insecurity, but with hunger. I did not wait for a formal course. I simply decided that if writing was the fulcrum of influence, then I had to learn it. And I had to learn it fast.

That decision pulled me into a different kind of learning loop—the one that had nothing to do with degrees and everything to do with observation, imitation, experimentation and reflection. In the pre-Google world, learning was slow and physical. I hunted for books, waited for TV interviews to be telecast, bought video CDs of legendary campaigns, scanned through background stories of them, talked to advertising stalwarts and media messiahs at events, corridors, restrooms—wherever possible and studied internationally famed creative directors like they were living chapters of a textbook. From one I learned finesse; from another, the staccato rhythm of dialogue writing; from a third, the audacity that electrified a room; from a fourth, the minimalism that made words feel like clean steel. Every day after work, I sat and watched, rewound, re-watched; read and re-read. Not to copy them but to decode them. Slowly, I felt my own voice emerge, shaped by many influences but constrained by none. That was my first experience of true meta-learning: the ability to learn the patterns behind the skills.

If writing was the craft, the industry itself was the melting pot those days where all creative forms were cooked—creative ideas, design excellence, art and aesthetics, music, script writing, film making, branding, marketing, behavioural studies—all of it. And above all, advertising had no patience for linear learning or fragile egos. A single day often required me to move from Indianizing a McDonald's product advertising to debating Samsung washing machine's design priorities; from giving Kurkure its *"tedha medha"* personality to refining the ecstatic *chatkara* of Hajmola candy commercial; from crafting the honesty of Peter England to sweetening a mother's day recipe with dear old Milkmaid; and finally, switching time zones to wrap up the night with a global brief for Compaq Presario laptops. just before calling it a day. Without Google, without Canva, without ChatGPT—we had only our minds, our teams, our curiosity and the brutal clarity of the brief. We had to understand the product, the market, the culture, the psyche, the behaviour of people before dinner. Looking back, I realize that this was meta-learning in its purest form: rapid cross-domain learning, high-pressure adaptation and constant updating of mental models. We were not just learning skills; we were learning how to learn.

What I did not understand then—but recognize now—is that these experiences trained the exact cognitive flexibility that today's AI-driven world demands. Meta-learning was not a theory for us. It was a survival instinct. Every campaign forced us to unlearn something old and absorb something new. Every client demanded a shift in tone, empathy or perspective. Every product required a new mental model. Advertising pushed us into concurrent learning, parallel thinking and perspective-switching long before those words became fashionable. And it did so without mercy, but with unexpected generosity. It taught us that when learning is not a task but a habit, growth is continuous and limitless.

Within a year, I was an art director who wrote his own copy. Within three years, I became the creative director of a branch of India's largest advertising agency. Not because I knew more than others, but because I learned faster than I believed I could. This was not talent; it was meta-learning. It was the steady compounding of small lessons, micro-skills, cross-disciplinary exposure and endless curiosity that further drove me to study behavioural sciences and design thinking—the only reason for which I am writing this book today. In the age of AI, I see the same principle returning with even greater urgency. Today, anyone can access information. But only those who can learn how to learn—adaptively, ethically, reflectively—will thrive.

And that, ultimately, is what I have been trying to say in this chapter. Artificial intelligence will learn faster than us but it cannot choose what to value. It cannot choose what matters. Humans are still the architects of meaning, direction and intent. To grow together with AI, we must cultivate a meta-learning mindset that is flexible, humble and ethically awake. My early years in advertising taught me this truth long before AI entered the picture: the most powerful skill is not what you know, but how you keep learning to grow continuously. The learning loop has been a lived experience for me. And as the world accelerates towards an AI-driven tomorrow, this ability to learn, unlearn and relearn will be the most human— and the most futureproof skill we possess.

BUILD AND EXERCISE THE ETHICAL MUSCLE

Developing Empathy and Imagination as Critical Design Tools in the Age of AI

How personal values, empathy and ethical clarity become our sharpest tools in navigating opaque algorithmic decisions.

In the fast-unfolding waves of artificial intelligence, few questions matter more than this: Who gets to decide what is right and what is wrong when the machine takes the call? This is not just a technical dilemma; it is a deeply human one. And it is not happening in the distant future. It is already here, encoded quietly into the systems that recommend our news, judge our creditworthiness, filter job applications and even influence our emotional state.

We are already surrounded by intelligent systems that interpret and influence our behaviour and often without our awareness. Algorithms curate what we see, what we buy, who we trust and even what we believe. But these algorithms are not neutral by nature; they are shaped by the values, data and design decisions of people. Which means, at their core, they are more than just systems of logic. They are systems of ethics—unspoken, untested and often invisible.

Fei-Fei Li, the visionary computer scientist behind ImageNet, and professor at Stanford University, has long insisted that we must keep AI "human-centred". For her, AI is not just a machine it is a mirror. A mirror that reflects our assumptions, amplifies our values and sometimes disturbingly exposes our blind spots. In this mirror, we see not only our potential but also our prejudices. It is for this reason that she repeatedly reminds us that the future of AI is not just about intelligence, but about wisdom. She observes, "I often tell my students not to be misled by the name 'artificial intelligence'— there is nothing artificial about it. AI is made by humans, intended to behave by humans, and, ultimately, to impact humans' lives and human society."

But what does wisdom mean in a world where conventional moral codes often lag behind technological possibility? Yuval Harari frames it differently. He does not merely ask what AI can do; he asks what it should do. He pushes us to question whether machines can or should inherit human ethics. And even more eerily, he wonders: When machines make choices on our behalf, whose ethics are they reflecting? Whose stories are they erasing?

Use the moral compass wisely

We once believed that ethics was something we could teach in philosophy class or encode in religious texts. But today, we face a new kind of moral dilemma as machines are making decisions at scale, in milliseconds, without context or conscience. And these decisions are not trivial. They affect real people. They decide who gets hired, who gets health care, who is watched and who is ignored.

Let us use an example. Imagine a hiring algorithm trained on decades of company data. If the company historically favoured male engineers over female ones, the algorithm might learn to do the same, not out of malice but out of pattern recognition. To the machine, it is just math. But to a human, it is injustice in statistical clothing.

Or think of a content moderation on social media. What gets taken down? What gets promoted? These decisions are often automated, driven by models that lack cultural nuance or historical sensitivity. A political dissident in one country may be flagged as a threat, while hate speech in another may be overlooked entirely. Again, these are not bugs; they are the result of value choices made upstream, often without debate or scrutiny.

It is necessary to cultivate our ethical compass because machines are augmenting decision-making in ways that blur lines of responsibility, empathy and judgement. In a world driven by code but bereft of universal moral guidelines, our personal clarity becomes our most critical survival skill.

It is no longer enough to ask, "Does it work?" We must now ask, "Is it right?" And not just from a technical standpoint, but from a human one. Does it protect dignity? Does it foster fairness? Does it respect the diversity of human experience?

And here is the deeper truth: in a world of algorithmic decisions, ethics is no longer solely a question for philosophers. It is a daily act of participation. If you are a designer, an engineer, a policymaker, or even a user, you are already part of the ethical equation. Whether you question the systems you use or blindly accept their outcomes determines whether you are shaping the future or being shaped by it.

Think of our ethical compass like muscle memory. If we ignore it, it atrophies. If we engage it regularly, it strengthens. We must ask ourselves: What would I do if this system failed someone I care about? Would I still trust it? Would I still defend it?

The ethical choices we make today—not in the distant future—will define the trajectory of AI for decades to come. We cannot delegate moral clarity to machines. Nor can we delegate it to corporations or governments without asking hard questions. We must step forward and become ethical co-pilots in this technological journey.

So the question isn't just whether AI can be trusted. The real question is: Can we be trusted to design and deploy it wisely?

And the answer starts with you.

Reject the myth that objectivity lies in code

We live in a world increasingly governed by algorithms that recommend what to watch, whom to hire, which routes to take and even how justice is administered. And because code is grounded in mathematics and logic, it is easy to assume it is objective but this assumption is a dangerous illusion. Algorithms are like cats: they do exactly what they want, and just pretend you are in control.

Code is written by people. Algorithms are trained on data. And data is a fossil record of human decisions, shaped by power, prejudice and policy; it is anything but pure. If society is biased, the data will be biased. And if the data is biased, the algorithm will be too, no matter how sophisticated it is.

When entertainment platforms began using AI to decide which trailers to promote, many noticed a strange skew: the algorithm kept favouring shows with high initial engagement—even if the engagement came from heavy marketing spends rather than genuine viewer interest. Because the AI was trained on past viewing and click-through patterns, it began amplifying only those titles that had historically received the most promotional push. Smaller, independent or experimental shows—despite strong storytelling— were quietly pushed downward in visibility. The algorithm was not choosing quality; it was inheriting the industry's longstanding bias towards big-budget content and scaling it. Once again, the system wasn't making a judgement—it was merely replicating the patterns buried in the data it was trained on.

The same applies to predictive policing models, healthcare triage tools and loan approval engines. These systems are efficient not because they are fair but because they learn what has worked before. They inherit society's past as if it were a blueprint, not a warning.

This makes algorithmic bias especially insidious. It does not feel like a decision is being made. It feels like math. It feels neutral. But neutrality is often the mask worn by systemic inequality.

And here is the deeper danger: these systems are automated, scaled and invisible. They operate in the background. They don't argue. They don't explain. They just deliver results quickly, silently and without accountability.

This should unsettle us. Not because machines are evil, but because their mistakes are so hard to see and even harder to trace. When an algorithm denies someone a job, a loan or a hospital bed, who is responsible? The coder? The manager? The training data?

Since the responsibility becomes distributed, it becomes diluted. So what should we do?

First, we must reject the myth that objectivity lives in code. Algorithms are not oracles. They are opinions embedded in mathematics. They reflect the assumptions, priorities and blind spots of their creators. Recognizing this does not weaken their usefulness; it makes their use more ethical.

Second, we must expand the circle of ethical responsibility. You don't need to write code to be implicated in its impact. If you deploy, endorse or benefit from algorithmic systems, you are part of the moral loop. And to know whether a bias has occurred, you must examine the outcomes: when a system's decisions consistently privilege some groups, ideas or possibilities over others without a clear rational basis, bias has already taken root. Business leaders, designers, product managers, policymakers have a role to play.

Third, we need visibility and explainability. Systems that affect people's lives must be auditable and understandable. Black-box algorithms may be efficient, but they are unacceptable when lives are at stake.

Lastly, we need humility. We must admit what we don't know and what machines can't know. Empathy, justice, dignity are not just edge cases. They are the essence of what technology should serve.

Objectivity is not found in code; it is found in conscience. And it is the responsibility of every individual in this new world to ensure that behind every algorithm, there remains a human heart awake and alert.

How to use our values as a strategic asset

For decades, organizations were taught to keep values and strategy in separate boxes. Values belonged in the mission statement; strategy belonged in the spreadsheet. One was for inspiration and the other for execution. But in the age of automation and algorithmic power, that distinction is crumbling fast.

In this new landscape, values are not just about identity they are about navigation. They aren't just personal principles; they are organizational tools. They shape choices in design, data governance, stakeholder engagement and market positioning. In fact, they may be the only compass reliable enough to steer through the fog of AI ethics.

Why? Because automation moves fast—faster than laws; faster than regulations; faster than public understanding. In that velocity vacuum, values fill the gap. They help answer questions before the courts can: Should we launch this? Should we pause? Who might get hurt?

Consider facial recognition—a technology capable of identifying a person in a crowd, unlocking a phone or tracking movement across cities with breathtaking speed and equally breathtaking risk. Some tech giants rushed to deploy it, chasing government contracts and investor approval. Others hit pause; as IBM did when it withdrew its facial recognition products, or as Microsoft did when it refused to sell the technology to police departments, citing concerns about racial bias, privacy and civic harm. Guess which companies now hold more trust among users, media and civil rights advocates?

Trust in this era is not just reputation; it is capital. It has an impact on hiring, retention, investment and partnerships. And trust is built not by saying the right things but by doing the right things when no one is watching.

Our values must show up in our decisions, defaults and error messages. And also in what data we collect and what we choose not to, in who is invited to the table when systems are designed and who is forgotten. Think of public institutions that digitize welfare distribution: when they design forms only in the dominant language or exclude those without smartphones, they embed a silent bias long before any algorithm begins to run.

The companies of the future will not just be AI-native. They will be ethics-native. They will design with empathy and audit for fairness. They will publish model cards, bias reports and social impact assessments as strategic rituals, not as PR moves.

And this shift is personal too. Our individual values—what we are willing to stand for, and what we quietly oppose—will be part of our professional signature. Silence is no longer neutral. In the ethical economy, inaction is a kind of voting.

This means we must learn a new fluency, not just technical literacy, but ethical clarity; not just design thinking, but consequence thinking; not just how to build but how to care.

Values are no longer soft traits; they are our edge.

Because as technology gets more powerful and more accessible, the question won't be: What can we build? It will be: *What are we building it for?*

And the answer, increasingly, will determine our place in the future.

Ask the ethical questions

Too often, ethical concerns are raised too late, that is, after a product has shipped, after the headlines break, after the harm is done. Why? Because questioning the moral implications of technology is still seen as slowing things down. It is treated like a speed bump on the road to innovation, not a steering wheel.

But what if we flipped the equation?

What if we saw ethical imagination as a core design capability, not an obstacle? A competitive advantage, not a compliance form?

This is what thinkers like Li and Harari are both calling for in different languages. While Li advocates for human-centred AI, where empathy is embedded in engineering, Harari urges us to remember our deep histories, to understand that intelligence without wisdom is dangerous. Together, their message is clear: ethics cannot be retrofitted. It must be integrated from the start.

And that begins with you.

Silence is not neutral; it is a design choice. The decision not to raise a question, not to surface a concern, not to speak up has consequences. Every product built without reflection carries the imprint of that absence. Algorithms trained without scrutiny don't just repeat bias—they repeat indifference. And when interfaces are designed without thinking of people's needs, like apps that lock out anyone with slow internet or poor eyesight, they don't just confuse users—they make them feel invisible.

We need new rituals because creating time and space for ethical reflection must become standard practice. Just as we budget for testing, marketing and scaling, we must budget for ethical inquiry. Not as a checkbox exercise, but as a breathing part of the process. Teams must be encouraged and rewarded for raising hard questions, for pausing in moments of doubt, for asking: *should we*, not just *can we?*

Because here is the truth: ethical tension is not friction; it is foresight. A culture that treats ethical thinking as a burden will repel talent and lose public trust. But a culture that treats ethics as a source of innovation—as a way to build deeper, more sustainable relationships with users and society—will lead with confidence and care.

The future is not just a technological frontier; it is a moral one. And silence will not protect us there—voice, vision and values will.

Be an ethical professional

We are entering a new chapter of professionalism the one that blends emotional intelligence with ethical discernment. In this rapidly evolving landscape, the most valuable professionals of the future will not be those who simply understand the intricacies of AI or technological advancements. Rather, they will be the ones who grasp the profound impact these technologies have on human lives, and who prioritize the ethical implications of their work.

To be that type of professional we must cultivate three critical habits:

Radical empathy: Technology should never be developed in a vacuum. While it is easy to become absorbed in the logic of algorithms and the structure of systems, the true measure of success lies in understanding the lived experiences of the people who will use or be affected by these systems. Radical empathy requires you to imagine, not just how the technology functions, but how it feels to those interacting with it. It demands stepping into their shoes by recognizing the complexities of their emotional, psychological and social worlds. Instead of relying solely on user personas or data dashboards, truly engage with the human element at every stage of design and deployment. For example, sit with an elderly person trying to navigate a hospital app on a cracked phone—one minute of that experience will teach you more than a hundred metrics ever can.

Curated scepticism: In a world driven by automation, it is crucial to ask questions about how and why decisions are being made. When choices are delegated to code, there is an inherent risk of overlooking ethical considerations. Curated scepticism involves scrutinizing assumptions, identifying biases and ensuring that systems are transparent. Don't accept the "default" answers at face value; challenge the status quo and know when to hit pause on the relentless push towards automation. A well-considered approach to scepticism prevents unforeseen harm and ensures accountability in technological development.

Moral rehearsal: Ethics cannot be an afterthought. Instead of reacting to issues as they arise, proactively consider the potential harm your designs or decisions might cause. Moral rehearsal is about anticipating negative outcomes and addressing them before they happen. Unlike curated scepticism, which questions ideas from the outside, moral rehearsal requires stepping inside the system and imagining the real consequences of its actions before they unfold. Run through various ethical scenarios and ask difficult questions—What might go wrong if the system is misused? What does the design simplify, and what does it complicate for users? By foreseeing challenges, we create space for more responsible decision-making.

These are not merely "soft skills". In a world where the speed of communication can either elevate or destroy reputations with a single tweet, and where technological harm can scale exponentially, ethics are not optional. They are survival skills. The professionals who demonstrate ethical leadership, who consistently choose to put people before profit or convenience, will be trusted and not left behind. And in this new era, trust will be the most valuable currency.

Reflect, adapt, evolve

There will never be a fixed rulebook for the age of AI because the terrain is too volatile. Innovations advance each other. What is groundbreaking today becomes outdated tomorrow. In such a fast-shifting landscape, rigid policies alone won't guide us. But what we can develop is something more agile, more human: ethical muscle memory.

Think of it like this: just as we don't learn to stay balanced on a bicycle by reading the manual, we don't learn ethics by memorizing codes. We improve our balance by riding, falling, adjusting and trying again. Ethical resilience works the same way. It comes from practice, discomfort and continuous questioning.

Building ethical muscles means deliberately exposing ourselves to complexity. It means reading stories about technologies that backfired not to feel superior, but to understand how small decisions lead to big consequences. It means engaging in uncomfortable debates, especially with people who see the world differently. It means asking, *What am I missing? Whose voice isn't in the room?*

It also means resisting what technology gently nudges us towards: the defaults. Most tools are designed for scale, not sensitivity. The settings we are handed—whether in algorithms, dashboards or metrics—are rarely neutral. The ethical professional knows this. They understand that every toggle switch carries weight. Choosing one variable over another and prioritizing speed over context, convenience over transparency are not merely technical decisions. They are ethical ones.

And the habit of reflection? Well, that is our gym. Every time we pause to ask, *What could go wrong?* Every time we challenge a metric or flag a concern—that is a rep. It doesn't make us perfect. But it makes us prepared. Over time, those micro-reflections form a reflex: a way of seeing the world that is both sharper and softer. Sharper in its awareness of consequence. Softer in its humility.

This is how ethical fluency grows; not from handbooks or compliance trainings, but from real engagement. We don't just follow the rules; we live the questions. We need to transform ethical uncertainty into an invitation to reflect, adapt and evolve.

In the end, the future belongs to those with strong ethical reflexes. Not because they have the answers, but because they have trained themselves to ask better questions.

In the AI age, living with better questions is not indecision—it is wisdom.

In the AI-driven world, we will not always have clear-cut answers. In fact, the answers we seek will often change as technology evolves, as social contexts shift and as our understanding of the potential consequences deepens. As the technology we create moves faster than we can predict, our commitment to this process of questioning must become our anchor, ensuring that we never lose sight of the larger ethical picture.

Ethical leadership in this new era does not come from possessing all the answers; it arises from curiosity and the courage to admit, "We don't know yet." It comes from the resolve to pause, reflect and explore the unknown with humility. Because, in the end, the intelligence we design—whether human or machine—must remain tethered to empathy. Furthermore, empathy is not something that can be coded into algorithms rather it must be nurtured, cultivated and experienced through compassion, understanding and shared humanity.

In this long-term journey, where every answer uncovered leads to even more insightful questions, and every step forward is made with the knowledge that we are shaping a future built on care, compassion and responsibility.

If we do not take ownership of our ethical role, we risk becoming bystanders in a world shaped by decisions we did not question. But if we nurture our ethical compass through empathy, imagination and intentionality we stand a chance of steering both technology and society towards a future that is not just intelligent, but humane.

How I learned it

Long before the world began speaking about AI ethics, algorithmic bias, or human-centred design, I found my earliest training in ethical imagination in a place most people never associate with moral seriousness: advertising. It still surprises me how deeply those years shaped my conscience. We tend to think of advertising in terms of glamour, punch-lines and persuasion. But beneath that veneer lay a much more demanding discipline—one that required imagination, responsibility and a constant attunement to human emotions. Looking back now, I realize that my ethical muscle was formed in those exact moments when we had to decide not just how to sell something to someone, *but how not to hurt anyone who is not that someone.*

In those pre-Google, pre-AI days, the work was slower, deeper and far more human. When we crafted a marketing strategy or a product launch campaign, after defining the target audience, the very next thing we always did was define who was *not* the target audience. We were trained to understand the people just outside the circle: the aspirational, the excluded and the unseen. You could create a premium product aimed at high-earning consumers, but those days for us it was unacceptable to design a campaign that punched the others in the face with the message: "This is not for you."

This discipline—this deliberate act of imagining those who would *not* buy the product—was my first encounter with what this chapter calls radical empathy. We had to feel the emotional and social worlds of people who were not paying our bills. We were required to anticipate how they might interpret a message, how it might affect their sense of dignity, and how it might shape their relationship with the brand and with themselves. Without knowing it, we were practising moral rehearsal long before the term existed in my vocabulary.

These choices were not small. They influenced the way multinational corporations understood India's complexity. Time and again we insisted that segmentation should never become exclusion. That a large corporation must have offerings that respect every economic band, every aspiration tier, every possibility of dignity.

And we saw that philosophy slowly take shape in the market itself. The day ITC came up with a Vivel for a Fiama, or when Godrej balanced Cinthol with Godrej No.1, or when Tata created Tata Agni for a Tata Gold, it felt like a quiet validation—proof that ethical imagination could shape not just communication, but entire product ecosystems. We had helped build portfolios where every Indian, regardless of city or salary, could find something with their name on it. That was empathy operationalized into strategy; dignity translated into design.

Then came the internet, the social platforms and the sudden collapsing of distances between metro sophistication and small-town sensitivities. Suddenly, we were not only learning the language of urban aspiration but also learning the emotional grammar of semi-urban and rural India. And again, the ethical questions returned, every day, in every brief:

How do we ensure people don't feel belittled?

How do we celebrate their reality with pride instead of trying to overwrite it?

How do we honour their identity while still inviting them into something new?

We responded with storytelling that was both bold and respectful. We glamorized the humble tea-slurping sound on national TV, not as a joke, but as a cultural truth. We created the iconic Hajmola Chatkara, not as a marketing gimmick, but as a tribute to the playful spirit of rural India. We designed communication that did not talk *down* to people but reached *out* to them. These campaigns looked simple on the surface, but they were built on a thousand tiny ethical decisions: whom to include, whom to respect, how to portray, what not to say, where not to cross the line.

It is only now, in the era of AI, that I understand how profound those lessons were. Without knowing it, we were learning the same ethical frameworks that this chapter argues for: radical empathy, curated scepticism, moral rehearsal and intentionality. We were trained to imagine how people might feel, even when they were not in the room. To anticipate harm before it happened. To design with conscience instead of convenience. To treat creativity as a responsibility, not a trick.

Those years taught me something essential: ethics is not a grand declaration—it is a daily habit. It is built through hundreds of small decisions, humble questions and quiet acts of restraint. And now, as AI systems start influencing who gets a loan, who gets care, who gets visibility, who gets heard the stakes have grown unimaginably larger. The same ethical vigilance that shaped our advertising decisions must now shape our technological decisions.

If I learned anything from those early days, it is this: empathy is not a soft skill; it is a design tool. Imagination is not a luxury; it is a compass. And ethical awareness cannot remain theoretical—it must live in every choice we make, every system we build, every message we release into the world. Advertising taught me that long before AI arrived. Today, I see it more clearly than ever. If we do not exercise our ethical muscle, someone else—or something else—will write the script of our collective future. But if we nurture it with empathy, imagination and courage, we can help shape a world where technology grows bigger, but humanity grows deeper.

MASTER THE INTERFACE

Every Job Will Soon Be a Tech Job

How we must become "interface fluent" between domain expertise and AI systems.

Developing interface fluency

For most of the modern era, jobs were built like silos. A teacher knew how to teach. A doctor diagnosed and treated. A banker managed risk. If we needed someone to build software, we hired a programmer. Technology was a department, not a dimension of every role.

This made sense in a world where digital systems were separate tools external to our jobs and optional in how we used them. They supported our work; they didn't shape it.

But something profound has changed.

Today, a cardiologist may begin her morning rounds by checking AI-assisted scans that detect early signs of heart disease better than her own trained eye. A farmer, once reliant on intuition and rainfall, now studies satellite-based soil analytics on his mobile phone to decide when and where to irrigate. A lawyer starts her day not with a human-written case brief, but with one generated by a legal artificial intelligence that has digested decades of court precedents in milliseconds.

We have crossed an invisible threshold where AI is no longer just a tool—it is becoming the interface, which is dissolving the long-standing wall between technical and non-technical domains.

What we are witnessing is more than just digitization. It is not automation in the old sense of replacing muscle with machine. This is a convergence of deep domain expertise with embedded intelligence systems that learn, predict and even decide. Artificial intelligence is not stepping into your job to replace you; it is stepping into your job to collaborate with you. Whether you thrive in that collaboration depends on your ability to be "interface fluent".

Interface fluency is not about coding and it is certainly not about becoming a machine learning expert or switching careers into data science. It is about learning to ask machines the right questions, interpret their answers and understand their limits. It is about knowing when a diagnostic AI is trustworthy and when its predictions may be skewed by flawed data. It is about being able to look at an output and ask: Does this make sense for my context, my clients, my patients, my community?

This is what makes interface fluency the new career currency. It is fast becoming the new literacy for professionals across sectors.

Andrej Karpathy, the former Tesla AI head, was among the first to describe this transformation with a new paradigm called Software 2.0. In his world, software is no longer written line by line by human engineers. Instead, engineers now curate datasets and train neural networks to learn the rules themselves. This flips the old hierarchy. Engineers become teachers of machines rather than mere rule-makers. In this world, the power lies not in coding brilliance but in the human intuition to sense when the AI has learned the wrong lesson.

Software 1.0 was written by humans.

Software 2.0 was learned by machines.

Software 3.0 is when the entire software development process itself becomes intelligent.

—Andrej Karpathy

Karpathy's team at Tesla did not just create self-driving algorithms. They cultivated machine learning systems that could learn from billions of real-world driving decisions. These systems, guided by engineers who understood both traffic dynamics and neural nets, started to approximate not just what a driver does, but what a good driver should do. That is interface fluency in motion.

Another visionary, Andrew Ng, who led AI teams at Google Brain and Baidu, has consistently argued that "AI won't replace you. But someone using AI will." His focus is on augmenting professionals, not eliminating them. In healthcare, for instance, Ng imagines a world where radiologists no longer scan every image, but instead validate diagnoses made by high-accuracy systems— freeing them to spend more time with patients. In manufacturing, he sees factory managers who no longer rely on spreadsheets, but who converse with predictive models that spot inefficiencies before they cause losses.

The transformation Ng envisions is not passive. It demands re-skilling, empathy for machines and a willingness to reimagine our jobs. And it demands a professional humility: accepting that AI will see things we won't, but also knowing that we must be the final judge of what should be done.

So what does this mean in practical terms?

It means that we are entering an age where the interface becomes invisible, yet utterly central across professions, from design to logistics to public health. We won't log into a system; it will meet us in our workflow. Algorithms will sit quietly behind every medical report, every classroom dashboard, every logistics chain. Our job will be to speak its language, not fluently but functionally. Not as a coder, but as a fluent translator between human complexity and machine precision.

This is why interface fluency is not just a technical skill, it is a cognitive one. It requires curiosity, critical thinking and the courage to work in ambiguity. It also demands a new kind of ethical responsibility because when machines are amplifying our decisions, our blind spots can scale just as fast as our insights.

This fluency is not optional. It is not a nice-to-have for tech-forward companies or digital-native teams. It is the new baseline for *all* organizations. Whether you work in a hospital, a court, a school, or a nonprofit if you don't engage with the AI embedded in your tools, someone else will. And they will make better decisions, faster and with greater impact. An NGO that uses AI to analyze local health patterns, for example, can identify high-risk communities weeks before field teams see the symptoms, allowing them to deploy interventions earlier and save far more lives.

To be clear: no one is asking a teacher to become a data scientist. But a teacher who understands how AI systems are identifying students who are at risk will be the one to change lives.

The boundary is gone. The walls are dissolving. The professions that once felt safe from the reach of AI, like nursing, education, law, agriculture, are now becoming its most promising frontiers. And the people who will lead this transformation will not be the ones who write code. They will be the ones who can listen to machines, question their outputs and translate their intelligence into human good.

The invisible interface is here. Can you see it?

Interface fluency is the new literacy. It is no longer a matter of whether we need it, it is how fast we can develop it. And in this new world, the ability to speak both languages—the language of our craft and the language of AI—will determine who thrives and who struggles.

Why AI fluency is the new communication skill

In the twentieth century, being bilingual in English unlocked doors in business, diplomacy and education. Today, a new language is emerging of patterns, predictions and probabilities, not nouns and verbs. This century will belong to those who are fluent not just in human languages, but in machine reasoning. AI fluency is the new communication superpower.

No, this does not mean everyone needs to become a software engineer. We do not need to know how to write algorithms or debug neural networks to thrive in an AI-powered world. We just need to understand how these systems behave. Just like drivers don't need to build engines but must understand road rules, AI fluency is about functionally interacting with intelligence by knowing its strengths, blind spots, tendencies and limits.

Think of it like driving in a foreign city. If we are unfamiliar with the norms, signs and terrain, we might survive but won't thrive. But if we understand the local language even a little we can navigate more confidently, collaborate better and make smarter choices. Likewise, when we understand how intelligent systems think, we gain agency. We stop being a passive user and become a strategic partner.

This bilingual advantage is already redefining professions previously considered "non-technical."

In tourism, a travel consultant fluent in AI can use predictive tools to anticipate crowd patterns, personalize itineraries and ensure travellers experience destinations in more meaningful, sustainable ways. In agriculture, a field officer fluent in AI can interpret satellite-based crop forecasts, identify early signs of pest outbreaks, and guide farmers towards timely interventions that protect both yield and livelihood.

Similarly, journalists who understand content recommendation engines don't just chase clicks they build integrity into virality. They can craft headlines that travel without distorting truth, understanding how algorithms weigh recency, sentiment and bias. They ask questions like: How will this be ranked? What assumptions is the machine making? Am I reinforcing echo chambers or bridging them?

E-commerce teams are facing the same shift. Imagine a category manager reviewing AI-generated product rankings. The model pushes a high-margin item, but her experience signals a mismatch with customer expectations. An AI-fluent manager does not reject or obey blindly—she questions the model's logic and ensures decisions serve both business and users.

The deeper implication is that AI is no longer just a tool—it is becoming a teammate, a collaborator, a mirror. That shift changes the human role entirely. We move from *doing the work* to deciding what gets done, why and how. Our value lies less in execution and more in judgement—in guiding the purpose, ethics and direction of intelligent systems. We become orchestrators of data, context, emotion and meaning.

This shift is already visible in the arts. The music industry, once considered purely human, now uses AI as a kind of digital co-composer. What is remarkable is not just speed, but emotional depth: listeners in several blind tests have rated AI-created compositions as "equally expressive" as human ones. The global AI in music market is projected to reach $3.4 billion by 2030, and nearly 40 per cent of commercial music may involve AI at some stage.

Tools like AIVA and MuseNet create orchestral scores on demand. Endlesss and Boomy enable musicians to co-compose rapidly. Holly Herndon performs with an AI "voice model" trained on her own vocals. Spotify now uses AI not just to recommend songs, but to generate mood-based soundscapes.

In 2022, an AI-generated song won a major composition contest in Japan—the judges chose it *before* learning it was AI-made. The controversy was not about quality; it was about authorship.

The point is not that AI replaces creativity—it expands what creativity can mean. But with that expansion comes responsibility. Someone must choose which outputs matter, which biases to guard against, which cultural signals to honour and where the human voice must lead.

This is why interface fluency matters. Whether you are a musician, marketer, teacher, NGO worker or journalist, your job will soon involve systems that think alongside you. You don't need to code, but you must know how to interpret, question and guide the machine. Because in this new world, the most important skill is not mastering AI—it is mastering the human judgement that directs it.

Modern marketers use AI not just to personalise communication, but to anticipate needs—reaching people with the right message at the moment when it is most emotionally and contextually meaningful. Architects are feeding AI climate data to co-design more sustainable buildings. In each of these fields, the people who rise are not the ones who fear machines but those who know how to talk to them, work with them and, occasionally, challenge them.

So the question for us is simple: Are we becoming bilingual? Are we cultivating the ability to understand how machines see the world? Not just how they work technically, but how they perceive, learn and act? Because in the coming decade, our fluency in this second language may determine our influence, our adaptability and our resilience in a world remade by intelligence.

Why you will become a designer of intelligence

In the industrial age, humans built machines. In the information age, we programmed them. But in the age of artificial intelligence, we train them, and that shift makes us curators more than creators.

To curate, in its truest sense, is to select with intent. Museums do it with artifacts. Editors do it with words. Now professionals across every industry must learn to do it with data. Because in AI, it is not just the model that matters; it is what you feed it. And that means everyone becomes a designer of intelligence, whether they realize it or not.

This is the central insight behind Software 2.0—the idea that instead of programming rules, we train systems with examples. And whoever selects those examples holds extraordinary power. A customer service chatbot behaves differently if it is trained on polite queries instead of irate complaints. A healthcare diagnostic tool offers different results based on the demographics and datasets it's exposed to. A hiring algorithm becomes fairer—or more biased— depending on the data used to teach it.

This is where the role of the curator-designer emerges. Unlike coders, curators don't write instructions. They shape intelligence through selection, context and curation. They are part strategist, part ethicist and part anthropologist. Their job is not only to optimize the machine's behaviour, but also to make sure that it aligns with human values.

Consider an HR professional tasked with training a résumé-scanning algorithm. She must decide: What counts as "potential"? Which experiences matter more? What signals suggest resilience, adaptability or leadership? In the process of selecting features, cleaning data and approving model behaviour, she isn't just building efficiency she is encoding a worldview. Every choice reflects a philosophy of talent, fairness and opportunity. The algorithm becomes a mirror of her moral compass, not just her technical choices.

The same is true for product designers, especially when the product itself has a personality. Imagine a team designing a smart fridge that suggests recipes based on what is inside. They must ask:

Should the fridge push healthier options first? Should it gently nudge you away from junk food at midnight? Should it prioritize budget-friendly meals for large families or gourmet ideas for food enthusiasts? If someone has very few items left, should the fridge recommend ways to reduce waste or prompt for donations? Each "design choice" becomes an ethical choice disguised as a UX decision—a quiet form of behavioural influence that shapes daily life.

Similarly, educators using adaptive AI tutors face their own version of this responsibility. When they upload lesson plans, adjust difficulty levels or approve reinforcement prompts, they are not just customizing content—they are shaping how the machine understands a child's curiosity, struggle and confidence. A simple tweak in pacing or reward style can encourage inquiry or quietly discourage it.

In each case—HR, product design, education—the pattern is the same: these professionals are no longer just *using* AI systems; they are shaping the values those systems will carry forward.

This isn't about making things pretty; it is about making things fair, transparent and purposeful. Curating an AI system is an act of storytelling. We are telling the machine what reality looks like, what success means, what matters. And in doing so, we are shaping how the machine thinks, learns and evolves.

But it is not just ethics. It is strategy. Companies that invest in thoughtful curation outperform those that don't. Why? Because curated systems are more relevant, more trusted and more adaptable. They serve humans better because they are trained by humans who understand complexity, not just efficiency.

This is why AI fluency alone is not enough; we need curation literacy. We need professionals who ask hard questions about inputs and think critically about edge cases. Edge cases are those unusual, rare or real-life scenarios that fall outside the "expected pattern"—the moments where a system is most likely to fail, misjudge or harm someone if we don't design for them. Who challenge feedback loops and seek diversity in training examples. In the future, our strategic advantage may come less from knowing how to "build" and more from knowing how to guide.

And that is the big idea: You don't just use AI—you design its worldview. Whether you are an analyst, a nurse, a coach or a policy expert, your ability to curate determines the machine's reality. And in a world run by intelligent systems, that is one of the most consequential forms of power we have ever had. Think of a sports coach feeding performance data into an AI assistant—if she emphasizes teamwork metrics over individual speed, the system learns to value cohesion, not just speed; she is literally teaching the machine what "success" means.

What interface fluency looks like on the ground

The most futuristic workplaces don't look like scenes from science fiction. There are no silver jumpsuits or blinking dashboards. Instead, they look surprisingly normal except for one big difference: the people know how to talk to machines. Not through lines of code, but through dashboards, prompts, dashboards, decisions. This is interface fluency, and it is transforming what work looks like on the ground.

In hospitals, for instance, doctors are learning to interpret AI-generated diagnostic suggestions—not to replace their judgement, but to augment it. A risk score for heart failure is just a number unless the physician understands how the model reached that conclusion. More importantly, they must know when to trust it and when to override it. This fusion of human and machine insight does not replace bedside manner. It deepens it.

In the legal world, junior associates no longer sift through paper stacks for hours. Artificial intelligence tools can now surface the most relevant precedents in seconds. But here is the thing: the machine can find the laws. It takes a human to interpret their meaning in context, foresee implications, and advise clients with empathy and wisdom. The new skill isn't data retrieval; it is nuanced translation. Let me share a few examples on how AI is influencing different industries.

Shoppers now get AI-curated product suggestions based not only on what they clicked, but on style patterns, past returns, climate, budget cycles and even upcoming festivals. An app might say, "Your monsoon wardrobe is incomplete—here are two options that match your past choices and today's weather."

Artificial intelligence travel guides are starting to map journeys that change in real time. If a traveller dislikes crowds, the system automatically shifts them to quieter routes or recommends hidden cafés and museums. If rain hits, the itinerary rearranges itself—like a smart companion who understands preferences better than a tour operator ever could.

And in media, interface fluency is perhaps most evident. Writers and content creators work hand-in-hand with real-time analytics, audience sentiment data and content optimization tools. The machine says, "This will work." The human must ask, "But *should it?*"

Ethical storytelling now depends on understanding how algorithms shape what stories are seen, shared or silenced.

Artificial intelligence can draft words, but it can't grasp the strategic "why" behind them. That is where humans come in. We don't just string words together, we shape narratives, connect with audiences and build trust. Artificial intelligence does not make that obsolete. It actually makes the human role more critical. Artificial intelligence is a tool, not a substitute. And just like any tool, its value depends on who is using it and for what purpose.

This shift isn't just about new skills. It is about new roles. The job market is beginning to reflect this hybrid reality. Titles are evolving; "data analyst" becomes "insight translator", "project manager" becomes "AI workflow coordinator". These are not buzzwords; they are reflections of how tasks are splitting between human and machine.

Hybrid capability is the new currency. That means comfort with ambiguity, fluency in systems thinking, and above all, the ability to see through the interface. Not just to interact with AI, but to shape its behaviour, refine its usefulness and challenge its biases.

The workplace of tomorrow will not ask: Can you code? It will ask, Can you think with code? Can you operate in a world where decisions are co-authored by human intention and machine logic? If so, you will not just be employable, you will be indispensable.

Futureproofing our careers

In a rapidly changing world shaped by technology, automation and AI, the old career model of static roles and fixed job descriptions is no longer sufficient to ensure success. The key to futureproofing our careers lies not in rigidly defining our roles but in cultivating dynamic fluency by becoming someone who can seamlessly navigate between different worlds, connect disparate concepts and translate complex ideas into accessible action. The future workforce will demand individuals who can bridge the gap between people and machines, between abstract goals and concrete systems, and between data and stories.

The importance of dynamic fluency

Dynamic fluency is the ability to operate across multiple domains, adapting and communicating across different contexts with ease. It involves not just technical competence but also emotional intelligence, cross-disciplinary knowledge and a deep understanding of how diverse systems interact. As AI continues to take over routine tasks, humans will increasingly be called upon to handle the complex work of connecting, translating and making sense of diverse information streams. The most in-demand professionals will be those who can collaborate with machines, understand their outputs and integrate those insights into human-centred strategies.

This doesn't mean that every professional needs to become a coder or a full-time technologist. The goal isn't to specialize in one singular domain but to develop a broad understanding of various systems—whether they be technological, organizational or cultural and how they intersect. Being a "boundary-spanner" or a "translator" means being fluent in the languages of different disciplines and being able to cross the boundaries between them to bring together diverse perspectives. In the modern workplace, the people who will thrive will be those who can function as connectors between traditionally siloed areas, facilitating collaboration and innovation.

The role of humans in a machine-mediated world

As MIT's Sherry Turkle observes, "Technology challenges us to assert our human values. Technology is not neutral—it forces us to confront the question of who we are and who we want to become." This reminder feels especially urgent in an age where machines can mimic our language, our choices and increasingly our creativity. Our real advantage, Turkle suggests, does not lie in out-performing machines but in deepening the qualities that machines cannot replicate: meaning-making, empathy, self-reflection and the ability to hold one another's stories. These human capacities—once nice-to-have—are becoming central to navigating a world where intelligence is shared across systems, sensors and algorithms.

As machines become more integrated into our professional and personal lives, the role of humans will be to provide the interpretative layer that translates data-driven insights into human-centric actions. Artificial intelligence can process patterns, but only humans can make sense of those patterns within the larger scope of societal needs, human behaviours and organizational goals. For example, AI can analyze consumer data, but it takes human insight to understand the emotional drivers behind purchasing decisions. Machines can optimize manufacturing processes, but it takes human creativity to design a new product that connects with consumers.

Let me cite a well-known case is Netflix's discovery of the demand for political dramas. Artificial intelligence noticed a growing pattern in viewer behaviour: audiences who watched British political shows were also rewatching American thrillers. The algorithm surfaced the insight, but it took *human interpretation* to recognize the emotional drivers behind it—a rising appetite for stories about power, secrecy and moral tension.

That human insight ultimately led to greenlighting *House of Cards,* a decision that transformed Netflix from a streaming service into a global content studio. The machine detected the pattern; only humans understood *why* it mattered and how to turn it into a cultural phenomenon.

Skills required for becoming a boundary-spanner

To thrive in the future, we will see ourselves as a boundary-spanner— someone who can fluently move between different disciplines and interpret knowledge across various domains. This role will not be confined to tech-savvy individuals alone. It will extend to every field, from marketing to education to healthcare. The power of translation is universal, as it allows individuals to connect and collaborate effectively across diverse teams, functions and industries.

To become an effective translator between worlds, there are several skills to cultivate:

Technical literacy

While we don't need to become an expert in every technical field, understanding the basic principles of emerging technologies like artificial intelligence, machine learning and blockchain will be essential. We must know how code speaks, that is, what it can do, what it can't and how it can be used to solve real-world problems. This will allow us to work alongside technologists without getting lost in the weeds of complex coding languages.

Cross-disciplinary knowledge

In a world that is increasingly interconnected, the ability to understand how different disciplines work and how they interact is crucial. Whether we are in finance, healthcare, education or marketing, we will need to understand how AI, data analytics and automation are reshaping our field. But equally important is the ability to understand the human side of our industry—the psychological, cultural and social dynamics that drive decisions and behaviours.

In education, many schools now use adaptive learning platforms that personalize lessons based on how students respond to questions. A teacher who understands only pedagogy may know how to teach, but a teacher with cross-disciplinary knowledge—someone who grasps both learning psychology and how the AI system interprets student behaviour—can intervene far more effectively.

For instance, when the system marks a student as "struggling," a cross-disciplinary teacher can recognize whether the student is actually confused, emotionally disengaged, experiencing cognitive overload, or simply clicking too fast. The AI sees the pattern; the teacher sees the *child*.

This blend of technological understanding and human insight is what allows educators to make nuanced decisions—adjusting the tool where needed and ensuring that the technology supports, rather than distorts learning.

Communication and storytelling

One of the most powerful tools we can possess is the ability to communicate complex ideas in clear, accessible ways. As a translator, we will need to take highly technical data and explain it in a way that resonates with non-experts. Storytelling will be an important skill for translating technical outcomes into human experiences—turning dry numbers into compelling narratives that inspire action.

In the publishing industry, editors increasingly rely on AI tools that analyze reader behaviour—identifying trends in pacing, genre preferences or even the emotional arcs that retain attention.

But these insights mean little unless someone can translate them into a compelling creative direction. A skilled editor acts as the storyteller behind the data: she explains to an author not that "chapter completion rates drop by a certain percentage in the middle", but that readers are losing emotional connection with the protagonist right when the stakes should rise.

She converts analytics into narrative guidance, helping the writer strengthen the story without drowning them in technical jargon. The machine detects the pattern; the editor communicates its meaning. That is translation in action.

Empathy and emotional intelligence

As AI continues to take over more of the technical, analytical and routine tasks, humans will be required to focus on what machines cannot do—understanding emotions, building relationships and navigating complex social dynamics. The ability to empathize, communicate effectively and collaborate with others will set humans apart in an AI-driven world.

Why translation is the future

Ultimately, the power of translation lies in its ability to align different stakeholders towards a shared goal. In an ever-changing world, where technological change is constant and the landscape can shift overnight, those who can act as translators between people, machines and systems will be best equipped to guide organizations through uncertainty and complexity. They will be the ones who create bridges between different worlds, ensuring that human creativity and machine efficiency work together to drive innovation and success.

Practice, reflection and curiosity will matter more than certificates.

Why every job will soon be a tech job (and why that is not as scary as it sounds)

If this chapter has taught us anything, it is this: the future does not belong to coders. It belongs to translators—people who can move effortlessly between the human world and the machine world.

To understand this, I often think of the pre-digital print publishing industry, which, in its own funny way, was one of the earliest training grounds for interface fluency. In those days, producing a book or a brochure was not a process—it was a pilgrimage. A manuscript moved from hard copy to transparent positive films. Films became plates. Plates became prints. Prints were cut, folded, stitched, bound, trimmed, packed and finally delivered. Every stage required a different specialist who spoke a slightly different language.

Designers spoke to plate-makers. Plate-makers spoke to machine operators. Machine operators spoke to fabrication teams.

And somewhere in the middle of that beautifully chaotic chain, the humble "translator" ensured nothing was lost.

Fast-forward to today: you hit "print," the machine purrs and out comes your final output—colour-corrected, aligned and ready to go. One click now replaces twenty conversations. And with AI stepping in, the decisions aren't just about *how* to print but *whether* to print at all. A production house or a marketing manager can soon ask an AI system: "Is this campaign better suited for online? Should this be a print-led launch? What is the optimal mix?"

And the system will analyze audience behaviour, budget efficiency, past campaign performance, even environmental impact and offer a recommendation.

But here is the twist: even with all that intelligence, the machine still needs someone who understands the brand, the audience, the cultural context and the emotional resonance. Someone who can translate machine insight into human meaning. That person is no longer a "tech" employee. That person is simply the modern professional.

The non-profit world is learning the same lesson—sometimes painfully. Traditionally, every major NGO project began with a baseline study. Then came phases of implementation, midline studies, learnings, corrections, more implementation, evaluation, and by the time the NGO truly understood the community—really understood them—the funding cycle ended.

The community changed, the landscape shifted, the problems evolved and yet the intervention was stuck in the original proposal document. The tragedy was not incompetence—it was timing. NGOs learned slowly because human systems reveal themselves slowly. And learning at that pace often meant the impact window closed before anyone could act on the insights.

Now imagine this cycle with AI as a partner.

Artificial intelligence can scan field notes, community chatter, local trends, weather shifts, health patterns and behavioural signals in real time. It can alert teams when something is changing—not after a midline survey, but after a week. It can tell project managers:

- This parenting workshop isn't landing well with young mothers.
- This livelihood training is gaining interest among older men.
- This village is showing early signs of seasonal migration.
- This behaviour is shifting much faster than expected.

What took NGOs two years, AI can flag in two weeks. What required endless field visits, AI can support through pattern recognition. What used to be "post-mortem learning" can now become "living learning."

But—and this is the pulse of the chapter—the NGO professional still must decide what the insight means, how it aligns with local emotions and what ethical implications it carries. Artificial intelligence can help us learn faster. But only humans can decide *what to learn from.*

And so, whether you are in publishing, nonprofits, sales, tourism, healthcare or agriculture, the message is simple: your job will soon be a tech job—not because you will code, but because your tools will think. Your role is to ensure they think *with* you, not *instead* of you. Your power lies in translating between community and code, between story and system, between what humans feel and what machines predict.

This is why interface fluency is not a technical skill. It is a human skill built on curiosity, empathy, integrity and imagination. And if we master this fluency, we don't just secure our career, we become the bridge that keeps technology aligned with humanity.

NEW AGE CO-CREATION

Making Machines Your
Creative Partners

*How human creativity combined with machine intelligence can
unlock breakthroughs in art, science and storytelling.*

The ancient myth of Prometheus stealing fire from the gods or
Leonardo da Vinci sketching his flying machines centuries before
aviation have one thing in common: the human urge to create. To
imagine what doesn't exist; to reach for something just beyond the
known. Creativity is an intrinsic part of our identity as humans.
Yet, as we stand on the threshold of the artificial intelligence era,
something profoundly new is unfolding. The spark of creation is
no longer solely held by humans.

In the past decade, machines have quietly crossed into territory once reserved for pure human imagination. Artificial intelligence now composes music, paints portraits, designs medicines and even drafts film scripts. We see this not just in experimental projects, but in genuinely acclaimed creative work.

The score for the HBO series *Westworld* used AI-generated variations to shape its haunting piano themes, allowing composers to explore musical patterns far beyond manual experimentation. By the early 2020s, short fiction and experimental narratives co-created with AI systems began appearing at international literary forums and writers' festivals, where they were discussed not merely as technological curiosities but for their narrative structure, originality and emotional coherence. This marked a decisive shift from AI as a gimmick to AI as a serious creative collaborator.

These milestones are not just curiosities; they reveal a deeper shift: creativity itself is becoming a shared space where human intention and machine imagination build on each other in ways neither could achieve alone.

At first glance, these feats might appear as little more than clever simulations—mechanical parlour tricks designed to imitate human creativity. But as we closely examine this phenomenon, we begin to see a different story unfold. This is not about machines replacing our creativity. It is about machines becoming partners in the creative process, working alongside us, amplifying our potential and often producing results neither could achieve alone. This is the dawn of a co-creative era where human intuition and machine computation blend together to create groundbreaking works of art, innovation and science.

Creativity is the quality that has enabled us to invent the wheel, paint the Sistine Chapel, and compose the greatest symphonies like Mozart's Symphony No. 41 and Beethoven's Symphony No. 9. It is the essence of what separates us from other species and, for a long time, what separated us from machines.

Yet, over the past several years, the lines between human and machine creativity have blurred. Consider DeepMind's AlphaGo, which did not just play the ancient Chinese game of Go and defeated a Go world champion but redefined how we think about strategy and intuition. AlphaGo's victory in 2016 wasn't just a triumph of machine learning; it was a demonstration of the power of AI to think creatively in a domain traditionally dominated by human expertise.

Similarly, the field of art has witnessed a similar shift. In 2018, a portrait created by an AI algorithm was sold at Christie's auction house for over $400,000, sparking debates about the nature of art and authorship. The portrait *Edmond de Belamy* was created by the Paris-based collective Obvious using a machine learning algorithm known as GANs (Generative Adversarial Networks). The AI used vast datasets of portraits from art history to generate its own vision of a portrait, blending classical techniques with an entirely new, machine-driven perspective. This brings us to ask a compelling question: If a machine can create art that resonates with us emotionally, what does that mean for the role of human creativity?

At the heart of these developments lies a fundamental shift in how we approach creation. In the past, humans were seen as the sole agents of creation, wielding tools and materials to bring ideas to life. But now, tools themselves are becoming co-creators. Artificial intelligence doesn't just respond to our commands; it helps us find new paths, generate unexpected ideas and explore dimensions of creativity that were once beyond our reach. The creative process is no longer linear, a simple sequence of human input followed by human output. Instead, it has become iterative and interactive, with AI algorithms offering suggestions, refining concepts and sometimes even making their own creative decisions.

This partnership between human and machine is not just confined to the arts. AI is helping researchers design new molecules for drugs, simulate complex biological processes and analyze massive datasets far faster than human researchers ever could. Demis Hassabis, the co-founder of DeepMind, has often spoken about the role of AI in advancing scientific discovery, particularly in fields like healthcare. DeepMind's work on protein folding, for example, represents a breakthrough in biochemistry, with AI algorithms solving a problem that had stumped scientists for decades. What is remarkable is not just that the AI solved the problem, but that it worked alongside human researchers, building on their understanding while pushing the boundaries of what was thought possible. "The best AI will be created by humans and machines working together," observed Hassabis recently.

This interplay between human intuition and machine calculation is at the core of the new age of co-creation. It is not about replacing human insight with machine precision; it is about enhancing human creativity with the computational power of AI. In fact, the more we examine these co-creative partnerships, the clearer it becomes that the human element is indispensable. Machines, no matter how advanced, still lack the depth of human experience, the ability to make intuitive leaps and the emotional resonance that often drives creative breakthroughs. It is in our capacity to dream, to connect disparate ideas and to feel deeply that we bring a unique richness to the creative process. Machines may be able to calculate, simulate and generate, but it is humans who imbue these creations with meaning.

The future of creativity, then, lies not in a struggle between human ingenuity and AI, but in a collaboration that amplifies the best qualities of both. Just as the first tools were extensions of the human hand, AI is now becoming an extension of the human mind. As we enter an era where creativity is no longer a solitary pursuit but a shared endeavour between human and machine, the question is no longer whether machines can create, but rather how we can best harness their power to unlock new realms of possibility and innovation.

As we move forward, the challenge will not be to resist or fear AI's creative potential, but to understand how to work alongside these machines in ways that push the boundaries of what we thought was possible. If we can embrace this new paradigm of co-creation, the future holds the promise of a new golden age of innovation, where human creativity is enhanced expanded and enriched by the collaborative intelligence of machines.

The death of the genius myth

For centuries, we have built myths around the solitary genius—the lone composer immersed in his studio, the scientist scribbling formulas on cocktail napkins in quiet cafes, the novelist secluded in a cabin battling the blank page. These stories of brilliance became part of our cultural DNA.

From Newton to Einstein, the genius was imagined as a unique figure who was isolated, intuitive and irreplaceable. But that myth is unravelling.

Today, innovation is not a monologue but a symphony. It is increasingly collaborative, collective and computational. The twenty-first century's most complex challenges like the climate change, synthetic biology, quantum computing cannot be solved by a single mind. They require interdisciplinary teams, open-source contributions, and now, the intelligence of machines.

Hassabis offers a compelling metaphor for our new era. He suggests we think of AI not as a rival, but as a "scientific collaborator". In 2020, his team stunned the scientific world when AlphaFold, an AI program of DeepMind, predicted the 3D shapes of proteins with astonishing accuracy, solving a grand challenge in biology that had persisted for half a century. This was not a victory of AI over human reasoning. It was a breakthrough enabled by the fusion of human curiosity and machine learning.

The rise of tools like AlphaFold, Copilot or ChatGPT does not signal the death of creativity instead it offers a telescope into complexity. Imagine Galileo without his lens, or Pasteur without his microscope. These were tools that extended perception. Artificial intelligence does the same but it extends cognition. It does not just show us more; it lets us see differently.

This shift challenges our narratives about genius. We must now recognize that many minds and many types of minds shape the future. A creative team might include a psychologist, a coder, a poet and a machine. What binds them is not a shared discipline, but a shared sense of inquiry.

In such teams, machines expand the scope of inquiry, model outcomes, test hypotheses, visualize data and suggest analogies. They free the human minds to focus on meaning, purpose and questions of beauty or ethics and not on rote calculations.

Indeed, the new genius may not be the one with the best idea, but the one who asks the most generative questions. Or the one who orchestrates the most productive collaborations between people, between ideas and increasingly, between humans and AI. The conductor of a creative ensemble may not write a single note but she enables the music.

To embrace this shift, we must rewrite our cultural scripts. The hero's journey may no longer be a solitary odyssey. It is now a dance between mind and model, intuition and inference, narrative and neural net. And new forms of creativity emerge in that dance.

So let us not mourn the myth of singular genius; let us celebrate its evolution. Because in the age of co-creation, a genius is no longer locked in a study. A genius creation is networked, distributed and often augmented. And in this new constellation of intelligence we are only just beginning to glimpse the light.

Why AI is a team sport

Creativity, for all its mystique, is not magic. It is a deeply human process including part intuition, part analysis, part perspiration. But at its core, creativity is combinatorial. We remix ideas. We borrow from the past to invent the future. We connect dots across distant domains.

Yet the human brain, magnificent as it is, has limits. It can only explore a handful of options before fatigue or bias sets in. Our imagination is bounded by memory, attention and prior experience. Enter the machine.

Artificial intelligence systems today can perform infinite iterations in seconds. A designer can input a few sketches or design prompts and the algorithm produces thousands of variations. A fashion artist needs to describe a mood or silhouette, and the model generates options drawn from global trends, historical garments and textile physics. What was once the slow work of trial and error is now a hyper-loop of iteration.

In architecture, firms like Zaha Hadid Architects use generative design tools to explore form and function in unprecedented ways. The human still chooses. But the range of possible solutions expands exponentially. Instead of drawing from five ideas, the designer draws from five thousand. That breadth allows for deeper curation.

In music, tools like AIVA or Amper don't replace composers they augment them. They provide scaffolds, suggest harmonies, evoke moods. A songwriter might use AI to generate a dozen chord progressions based on a desired emotional arc. Then she selects, tweaks and adds nuance. The machine proposes. The human disposes.

The new creative instinct is not just to produce, but to perceive patterns among abundance. The artist is no longer the sole maker. They are the interpreter, the conductor, the ethical guide. The one who says: "This version moves me. That one doesn't."

What does this mean for originality? Some worry that AI will make art formulaic. But history reminds us that tools shape style, not soul. The invention of the camera didn't kill painting. It sparked Impressionism.

How?

The advent of photography introduced a new way of seeing and capturing the world. It offered a different perspective that was more realistic and immediate than traditional painting techniques. This influenced Impressionist artists to experiment with new ways of depicting light, colour and form in their work. Photography was able to capture everyday scenes and moments, which inspired Impressionists to move away from historical or mythological subjects and focus more on contemporary life, landscapes and scenes of daily activities. The ability of the camera to crop and frame scenes in unique ways influenced Impressionists to experiment with unconventional compositions, such as off-centre subjects, unusual angles and close-up views.

The synthesizer didn't destroy music. It revolutionized the landscape of electronic music, fundamentally changing how artists create and express sound. Influential artists in electronic music have developed signature sounds that showcase the creative potential of synthesizers, often defining the aesthetics of their respective genres. When machines become partners, art evolves, not ends.

The shift towards a more inclusive and accessible approach to creativity is evident. A teenager in Lagos or Dhaka can now produce world-class design with free tools. The gatekeepers of creativity such as prestigious schools, elite mentors, expensive equipment are becoming less absolute. Iteration becomes democratized.

In this sense, creativity becomes not just about individual brilliance, but about inclusive possibility. More people can try. More ideas can surface. And in that vast field of iteration, something magical happens: the rare, the moving and the original emerge.

So yes, the machine can now generate beauty, but it is still the human who recognizes truth. The brush may be automated, but the touch—the signature—is ours.

Why the poet must consider the algorithm

Words have always been our most powerful instruments of thought. From ancient mythologies to modern manifestos, it is through language that we have shaped beliefs, cultures, identities and ideologies. For centuries, the written word held a singular authority. Books, essays and speeches did not just inform, they defined reality. To be articulate was to be intelligent. To be well-written was to be remembered.

But in the age of generative media, this hierarchy is dissolving. Language is no longer the final form of thought; it is the opening move in a larger multimodal conversation. Words now trigger images. Phrases manifest into videos. Descriptions morph into immersive 3D environments with nothing more than a few keystrokes. In this world, the word still matters but not because it ends the creative act. It matters because it begins it.

Prompt becomes palette. Sentence becomes scaffold. Text becomes trigger.

A captivating visual concept like a tiger walking through a neon-lit city at midnight no longer needs a painter or cinematographer to bring it to life. A machine does it in milliseconds.

In this world, the word still matters but not because it ends the creative act. It matters because it begins it. This transformation doesn't diminish language; it stretches it. Language becomes elastic, generative, spatial. Writers are no longer limited by text. They are directors, designers and world-builders—conductors of audiovisual symphonies rendered by code.

But this shift also challenges our assumptions about originality and intent. In generative spaces, meaning is not fixed; it is fluid. A phrase interpreted by one AI model may produce vastly different outcomes when rendered by another. Creativity is no longer just authored; it is co-shaped, iterated and modulated in real-time.

This repositions the role of the human creator. The storyteller is now also a systems thinker. The poet must consider the algorithm. The communicator becomes a prompt engineer, a syntax strategist, a semantic sculptor.

We are entering an era where *how* you say something determines *what* becomes possible to see, hear and feel. The word, once an endpoint of intellectual mastery, is now a starting point for multimodal exploration.

We must prepare the next generation of thinkers and artists to operate in this space not merely to write well, but to write wide. To think not just in paragraphs, but in possibilities. Not just in ideas, but in orchestrations of media that shift moods and perceptions instantly.

In this new landscape, literacy expands beyond text. It includes visual literacy, media fluency and an intuitive grasp of systems behaviour. And just as we once taught rhetoric to shape argument, we must now teach prompt craft to shape reality.

The creator as the curator of complexity

Traditionally, to create meant to craft something from start to finish with our own hands, tools and intellect. The artist painted every brushstroke. The composer arranged every note. The writer revised every sentence. Creation was synonymous with authorship, mastery and complete control.

But in the age of intelligent machines, this linear model of authorship is changing. The creator is becoming less of a lone maker and more of an orchestrator of human and machine potential. In this model, the value of creativity no longer lies only in execution, but in the ability to shape the process, curate the inputs and steer the outputs with intention.

Consider a fashion designer working with AI-driven pattern generators. Instead of sketching every silhouette by hand, the designer feeds the system fabric types, body forms, cultural inspirations, sustainability goals and colour palettes. The machine produces hundreds of unique design variations in minutes. The designer's brilliance is not in drawing each dress, but in framing the creative constraints, sensing which patterns capture an emerging cultural mood and elevating the machine's options into a coherent artistic vision.

This is not about laziness or outsourcing. It is about leverage.

It is about using intelligence—both human and artificial—as raw material. The creator becomes a systems integrator, a decision-maker, a curator of complexity. And this is no small shift. It moves creative excellence away from perfectionism and towards discernment.

In the past, mastery was about technical finesse. Today, mastery is about how you navigate, combine and interpret infinite possibilities. The question is no longer, "Can I do this myself?" but rather, "How do I design the system that lets the best solution emerge?"

This model also encourages co-creation. Teams across disciplines and time zones can interact with the same generative models in real time, refining prototypes, remixing ideas and iterating on outputs faster than ever before. The boundaries between creator and collaborator dissolve. So do the boundaries between creativity and strategy, intuition and data, idea and execution.

Yet this orchestration model requires a new type of literacy: design thinking as choreography, not just structure. Systems fluency as creative intelligence. Knowing which tools to summon, which prompts to issue and which iterations to explore has become the core skill of the modern creator.

We are no longer in the age of DIY or do-it-yourself. It is DIAI now—design it with AI.

Prompt literacy is the new design literacy

If design literacy once meant the ability to sketch, wireframe or prototype, today it also means knowing how to *converse* with intelligent systems. The rise of large language models, diffusion models and generative AI has introduced a new foundational skill to the creative process: prompt literacy.

A prompt is not just an instruction; it is a frame, a seed, a poetic constraint. In the hands of an expert, a prompt is a spell that summons new worlds. In the hands of a novice, it is just a query. Give an expert chef a single ingredient and they craft a gourmet dish; give the same ingredient to a beginner and you get something edible at best—prompts work the same way.

The difference is not in the tool but in the fluency.

Consider how an experienced prompt engineer can use subtle tweaks in phrasing, rhythm or metaphor to evoke radically different outputs. The same model can produce sterile mediocrity or breathtaking beauty, depending on the nuance of the prompt. This is not unlike how a skilled writer uses syntax or how a jazz musician plays with timing. It is *craft*, not code.

And yet, prompt literacy is not being taught at scale. Schools, studios and design firms are still catching up. The irony is stark: we have given everyone a symphony orchestra, but we have not taught them how to conduct.

Prompting well requires more than knowing the right keywords. It demands an understanding of how AI interprets language. It requires empathy for the machine's perspective. It rewards curiosity, experimentation and iterative thinking.

Just as graphic design evolved from static layouts to dynamic systems thinking, prompt literacy will evolve from simple command-giving to dialogue-making. Designers and storytellers will become sense-makers across modalities, fluent in constructing layered, cascading prompts that adapt across contexts and media forms.

Ultimately, prompt literacy is not about controlling machines it is about expanding human expression. It gives creators a new brush, a new stage, a new partner. And the future belongs to those who know how to dance with this partner gracefully, playfully and intentionally.

Reimagining originality

Originality once meant "first of its kind". It was defined by novelty—ideas never seen before, songs never heard, designs never built. But in the remix era, originality is no longer about invention from zero; it is about interconnection. About the surprising relationship between things. About *context*, not just content.

Consider the rise of sampling in music. Hip-hop did not devalue originality by reusing old beats; it redefined it. An R.D. Burman classic like "Kanta Laga" from the seventies is remixed with contemporary beats and pre-programmed tones is still finding teenagers as its audience, or a DJ looping a James Brown riff and layering it with contemporary spoken word, transformed the past into something radically present. Originality became relational—born in the gaps between fragments.

Now, generative AI amplifies this dynamic. Everything ever created—every image, song, film or phrase—is now data. A remixable ocean of styles, moods, formats and references. The creative act becomes less about making something from scratch and more about choosing what to combine, how to sequence, when to pivot and why to evolve.

This reframes the creator's role: who is no longer just the *maker* of things, but the *mapper* of meaning. His unique voice emerges not from isolation, but from his pattern of selection. His originality is not what he excludes—it is what he chooses to connect.

In this world, attribution becomes complex. So does ownership. But what becomes clearer is that creative genius is not about having the rarest ideas. It is about having the deepest relationships with ideas.

How to master the art of meta-cognition

In the age of infinite generation, the rarest skill is no longer output; it is self-awareness. When we can generate a thousand options in seconds, the true power lies not in making more, but in knowing why we are making at all.

Meta-cognition—the ability to think about your own thinking—becomes the artist's edge.

What are we trying to say? What values are embedded in our aesthetic? What does our prompt imply about our worldview? These questions are no longer philosophical luxuries. They are creative imperatives. Because the faster machines can generate for us, the more essential it is that we bring intention to the table.

Our sense of self—our aesthetic code, our ethical compass, our emotional clarity—becomes our signature. However, AI can simulate style, but it cannot simulate soul. And soul is what shows up when we know who we are, what we are here to express and how our creative choices shape the world we want to live in.

The new creative superpower is not output—it is inward insight. The future will not be led by those who produce the most. It will be led by those who know what matters most and how to use every tool, prompt and possibility to amplify that meaning. We are entering a future not of diminished humanity, but of expanded possibility.

How I learned it

My relationship with machines did not begin with AI models or generative tools. It began when I was a studying design. It began in a small design studio in the mid-nineties, when Adobe visited our design institute and introduced us to something that sounded almost magical—a software called Photoshop, then in its early, evolving stages. They wanted young designers, illustrators and visual thinkers like us to push its limits. Not to use it passively, but to break it, stretch it, challenge it and tell them what more it needed to do.

Until then, in India, "image correction" meant taking bromide prints to a fine artist's desk. A senior gentleman with impossibly steady hands would sit with tiny brushes and retouch grainy portraits. If we needed a background cleaned, a shadow softened or a wrinkle diminished, it meant hours of painstaking labour—and it always carried the warmth of human imperfection. Then suddenly, this software arrived with its odd palette of tools: clone stamp, healing brush, feathering, masking. With a few keystrokes and careful hand movements, we could do in minutes what earlier required days of craft. It felt as if a new door had opened into a different dimension of creativity.

Looking back now, I realize something profound: we were not just learning Photoshop—we were co-creating it.

Every time I layered an image, pushed the saturation too far or failed to clone cleanly, I was essentially telling the software: here is where you struggle. Here is where you must evolve. And this was happening with thousands of designers around the world. We were refining a tool that would one day refine us. We were feeding it our frustrations, our aspirations, our hand-crafted sensibilities. We were showing it the tiny nuances of human touch—the softness of a shadow, the intentional imperfection of a brushstroke, the emotional intelligence of composition.

And Photoshop learned. And so did we.

In hindsight, that period was my first true experience of co-creation—not the buzzword we use today, but a living practice. The machine was not doing my work; it was learning what mattered to me. Not replacing my skill, but amplifying it. Not reducing my creativity, but extending its reach. When I look at today's AI tools—Canva, Midjourney, generative models—I see the same lineage. I can even say, with some quiet pride, that designers of my generation helped shape this evolution. Our daily struggles became training data. Our instincts became design logic. Our visual language flowed into the early DNA of machine creativity.

But the lesson did not end with software. Years later, as I watched my children grow, I found myself reflecting on the same principle in an entirely different context. We don't shape children by dictating every move; we shape them by creating an environment worth absorbing. If we surround them with rich music—classical, semi-classical, timeless Bollywood melodies—they begin to reject shallow soundscapes on their own. If they grow up around good books, thoughtful films and textured conversations, they develop a natural appetite for depth.

And once that inner culture forms, they take it forward—into their devices, their choices, their future collaborations with intelligent machines. They begin to co-create with AI not from a place of convenience, but from a place of discernment. They bring taste, values, empathy and emotional texture into the technological space.

This is exactly what the chapter has been trying to say. The next generation will not simply *use* AI—they will *collaborate* with it. They will treat intelligent systems the way we once treated evolving tools: as partners, not replacements. But to do that, they need more than technical skill. They need emotional intelligence to sense nuance, philosophical grounding to ask better questions and ethical judgement to decide what only humans should decide.

And so, as I think about those early Photoshop days—the imperfect strokes, the broken tools, the moments of wonder—I realize that the biggest lesson was never about software. It was about environment. Machines grow when humans feed them meaning. Humans grow when machines expand their choices. But both grow best when the world around them is built thoughtfully with curiosity, empathy and cultural richness.

If we want a future where AI amplifies us rather than dilutes us, we must create co-creating environments in our studios, classrooms and homes. Places where imagination is not only taught but lived. Places where machines learn from our best and not our worst. Places where creativity is shared, not surrendered.

Because co-creation is not just the story of technology. It is the story of how we become more human in the presence of intelligent machines.

YOU ARE WHAT YOU FEED THE MACHINE

The Learning Curve Just Got Steeper

We built machines that reflect us. Now they reshape us.

The crumbling fortress of traditional education

For over a century, formal education has been the passport to professional success. The degree was a symbol of arrival. But today, that symbol is fraying. A college degree, once the gold standard of competence, is increasingly mismatched with the needs of a world transformed by artificial intelligence, automation and rapid global shifts.

The problem is not that education has failed entirely. It is that it has not kept pace. The modern workplace moves in quarters, not semesters. Industries are redefined in months, not decades. Yet many universities still teach with syllabi drafted before the iPhone existed. The software engineer who graduates with a four-year degree may find half of what they learned already obsolete. The business student memorizing case studies from the 1990s is walking into a workplace driven by real-time analytics and AI-powered forecasting.

As futurist Alvin Toffler warned, "The illiterate of the 21st century will not be those who cannot read and write, but those who cannot learn, unlearn and relearn."

In a world overflowing with information and accelerating change, the real currency is adaptability—the ability to distil what matters, discard what doesn't and re-skill without defensiveness or delay.

Andrew Ng echoes this sentiment but adds a pragmatic solution. He doesn't believe everyone needs to become an AI expert. But he does believe everyone needs to become AI-aware. His vision for accessible, modular AI education—what he calls "nanodegrees" or bite-sized, industry-relevant courses—aims to arm people not with credentials, but with competence. Ng once observed, "Education is not about thinning the herd. Education is about helping every student succeed."

Nanodegrees offer a faster, more flexible way to build real-world skills in tech, business and data science. These short, online programs focus on hands-on learning, so we can gain expertise and boost our career without spending years in school. Nanodegrees are becoming more popular, especially in tech and business industries, where employers value real-world skills over traditional credentials.

Why is this important? Because the job you were trained for may not exist in ten years. In fact, for many, it already doesn't. Taxi drivers now compete with autonomous vehicles. Radiologists work alongside AI that can spot tumors more accurately. Financial analysts rely on bots for real-time market insights. And even writers collaborate with language models.

Degrees were built for stability. Today, we live in volatility. Our diplomas won't adapt; we must. The modern worker needs a growth mindset and a re-skilling playbook that operates more like a gym membership than a graduation ceremony. You don't stop learning at twenty-one. You commit to staying fit—mentally, technically, creatively—for life.

Education must transform from being a fortress we enter once, to a tool-belt we carry everywhere. In this world, continuous learning is not a luxury—it is a survival skill. And those who thrive won't be the most credentialed, but the most curious.

Nanodegrees and modular learning—flexible, affordable and accessible alternatives to traditional education

Nanodegrees, short bootcamps, micro-credentials are no longer fringe ideas; they are the backbone of a new learning economy. As companies race to stay competitive in the AI era, they are increasingly interested in what we can do, not where we studied. Skills, not schools, are the new hiring currency.

Consider how the world of technology has embraced modular learning. Platforms like Coursera, Udacity, edX and Khan Academy offer focused, practical learning experiences that teach you one skill at a time—data visualization, Python for machine learning, UX design for mobile apps, prompt engineering for AI systems. They do this by breaking complex competencies into small, standalone modules—each designed to be completed in weeks rather than years. Instead of wading through an entire degree program, learners can target exactly what they need, practise it through real-world projects and apply it immediately in their work. These courses are often taught by working professionals or leading researchers. They cost a fraction of traditional tuition. And they evolve fast, reflecting current market needs.

Ng's AI for Everyone on Coursera is for marketers, managers, HR professionals and healthcare workers who need to understand how AI impacts their field. It introduces concepts like supervised learning, data labelling, model bias and ethical dilemmas without diving into the code. It is knowledge for the interface era.

The idea is not to learn everything. It is to learn just enough, just in time. This is "problem-first" learning. We don't study for a hypothetical job. We study because a real-world challenge requires it now. Got a project involving data? Take a two-week crash course in Tableau. Need to automate a workflow? Learn how to use Zapier or Python scripts. The learning is directly tied to our momentum.

Companies like Google, IBM and Accenture now offer their own nano-certifications. Even governments are catching on—Singapore's SkillsFuture initiative subsidizes citizen re-skilling. Germany's vocational education model is blending hands-on apprenticeships with digital learning. SkillsFuture is a national movement that was launched in 2015 to provide Singaporeans with the opportunity to develop their fullest potential throughout life, regardless of their starting points. Over the years, SkillsFuture continues to be the driving force for individual and enterprise-led upskilling and reskilling efforts to prepare our workforce for a rapidly evolving economy. In India, we have a similar comprehensive, government-led initiative called the Skill India Mission which is also known as the National Skills Development Mission. This too was launched in the same year.

The message is clear: learning must move from ivory towers to kitchen counters, bus rides, coffee breaks and lunch hours. Believe me I have lived this quite literally. During an UN disaster-risk reduction project in the Maldives, I once ended up learning how to climb a coconut tree during my lunch break simply because our local cameraman suddenly declared that his agency's safety policy did not allow him to climb it (despite the fact that he could scale it faster than a squirrel). With no other option, and with only one of us left who could handle the camera, I found myself halfway up a swaying palm tree, clutching a camera, a coconut and my dignity—all in the name of "learn quick, learn enough".

Nanodegrees also democratize access. We don't need $100,000 or four years of our life to become employable. We need Wi-Fi, curiosity and discipline. This has the potential to unlock a billion dreams—mothers re-entering the workforce, factory workers pivoting to logistics tech, farmers adopting AI-driven agriculture, students from villages in Assam learning prompt engineering.

We must embrace a learning culture that is fast, flexible and frictionless. Nanodegrees are the agile upgrade to an outdated operating system. They allow us to evolve our identity, not just our skills. You are not just an accountant anymore; you are a data-savvy finance strategist. You are not just a teacher; you are a blended-learning experience designer.

As modular learning becomes mainstream, we will stop asking "What's your degree?" and start asking "What can you build, solve, design, improve or rethink?"

AI fluency is the need of the hour

To thrive in the coming decades, AI fluency must be seen not as a specialization, but a general skill like reading, writing or using spreadsheets. It is no longer just the domain of tech elites. Whether you are a farmer or a fashion designer, a teacher or a truck driver, understanding the basics of AI will be essential.

But what does AI fluency mean? It is not the ability to code neural networks. It is the ability to understand what AI can and cannot do. It means knowing how algorithms make decisions, what data biases look like, when machine suggestions are useful and when they are dangerous. It means being comfortable asking AI tools meaningful questions and knowing how to interpret the answers.

Artificial intelligence is not a genie. It is a pattern recognition engine trained on massive datasets. It doesn't "understand" the world as we do. It doesn't feel, intuit or empathize. What it can do is uncover relationships between data points far faster than any human. What it can't do is know when those relationships are misleading, offensive or unethical.

This is why human supervision remains essential. In AI-enhanced medicine, the doctor is still responsible for the diagnosis. In algorithmic policing, the officer must still assess context. In automated journalism, the editor is still the guardian of truth. Artificial intelligence can suggest, accelerate and assist but the buck stops with us. For example, predictive-policing tools may flag a neighbourhood as "high risk" based on historical data, but a responsible officer must still judge whether the alert reflects current reality or simply old biases.

Artificial intelligence will power every industry, touch every profession and redefine what it means to be skilled. But like electricity, it can shock and burn if misused. We must all become AI-literate citizens not just to protect our jobs, but to protect our values.

Organizations should invest in AI onboarding programs the way they used to teach MS Office. Communities should run workshops on ethical AI use, especially in education and healthcare. Schools should introduce AI ethics in middle school. And NGOs working in hard-to-reach regions should train youth groups and women's collectives in data rights and AI applications for livelihoods. For instance, an NGO working in the flood-prone villages of Assam could train women's self-help groups to use simple AI-powered crop advisory apps. These tools can analyze soil moisture, predict rainfall and recommend the best time to sow seeds. At the same time, youth volunteers could learn how to protect community data on these apps—understanding what information should be shared, what shouldn't and how to spot manipulative platforms. In places where agriculture and livelihoods hinge on every decision, this kind of AI literacy can turn vulnerable groups into informed, empowered decision-makers.

AI fluency empowers us to be more than users. It makes us thoughtful co-creators. And in an age where machines learn from us, we must ensure they are learning the right things.

Lifelong learning is a mindset, not a task

We often think of learning as a staircase. We climb through primary school, reach college, maybe grad school and then we are done. But in truth, learning is a spiral. The world loops back, shifts direction and demands that we see old problems with new eyes. The future belongs to those who embrace this spiral.

Homo sapiens rose not because they were the strongest or the fastest, but because they could adapt. We could collaborate flexibly in large numbers, imagine new futures and revise our stories. Lifelong learning is simply an extension of that ancient strength.

But here is the catch: learning isn't always fun. It is often uncomfortable. It challenges our identity and exposes what we don't know. And yet, it is also liberating. It allows a fifty-year-old to master AI-driven supply chains. It helps a high school dropout build an app that changes lives.

At just twenty-six, Kishan Bagaria a school dropout sold his app for a staggering ₹416 crore! Kishan, who hails from Dibrugarh, Assam, always had a passion for tech gadgets. After self-teaching coding online, he founded texts.com, a revolutionary platform that integrates all messaging apps like WhatsApp, Twitter and Instagram into one dashboard. Developed in 2020, texts.com gained popularity through word of mouth. This innovative messaging app caught the eye of Matt Mullenweg, the owner of WordPress.com and Tumblr, he called Kishan a "generation tech genius", leading to an acquisition for $50 million. Kishan has moved to San Francisco in 2023 to further develop his platform. His journey from a school dropout to a tech mogul is inspiring young minds everywhere. Texts.com, under Automattic's ownership, has the potential to revolutionize how we manage our digital communication. Kishan Bagaria's story serves as a testament to the power of innovation and the boundless possibilities within the tech world. He showed that a college degree is optional to learn the skills when we have access to the internet.

It gives a war refugee the tools to teach herself web design and freelance across borders.

In this new world, the learner is not a passive recipient. They are a problem-solver, an explorer, a pattern-seeker. They google, they iterate, they build, they fail, they try again. They seek mentors, join online communities and treat feedback as fuel.

The reskilling mandate, then, is not just about employment; it is about dignity. It is about reclaiming agency in a world of flux. When we learn, we become less anxious. We feel more powerful. We are no longer just surviving change; we are shaping it.

We need new rituals for lifelong learning like peer study circles, community learning grants, corporate learning sabbaticals, skill-share festivals. Learning should be social, visible and celebrated, not hidden in late-night YouTube binges or quietly pursued massive open online courses (MOOCs) on Udemy, Coursera, etc.

Most importantly, we must decouple our identity from our degree. You are not your diploma. You are your curiosity, your adaptability, your integrity and your willingness to grow. That is the real CV of the future.

How I learned it

Long before the world began speaking about nanodegrees, micro-credentials or modular learning, I learned the power of real-time, self-driven education from someone who did not even finish the fifth standard. His name was Babu—a quiet, bright-eyed boy who worked in the canteen of our Bengaluru advertising agency in the mid-nineties. He must have been 14 or 15, an orphan, doing odd jobs to earn a living. He served chai and coffee twice a day to all of us, walking among celebrated creative directors, art heads and copywriters as if he were invisible.

But there was something unusual about him. Every time he crossed the glass door of the air-conditioned studio—the sacred space holding our shimmering Macintosh workstations—his eyes would widen. In those days, computers in ad agencies were treated almost like holy idols. Shoes outside. Silence. Limited access. Only the chosen few could enter that cold, humming temple of creativity. Yet, Babu would linger at the door for a few seconds longer every day, staring at the screens as though they were plates of hot biryani he could not yet taste.

One late evening, when I was still working and needed a coffee break, he came in with his usual wide-eyed awe. I finally asked him, "Why do you look at these machines like that?"

He whispered, "Because one day, I want to learn what you do on those TV sets." What he meant was the monitor. But what he really meant was *possibility*.

Fresh out of design school, high on social responsibilities and eager to teach, I told him, "Why someday? Come in now. Learn." And that evening became a turning point—perhaps for both of us.

Babu began coming in quietly during late hours, after his canteen duties. He did not want theory. He did not want lectures. He did not want to understand design principles or typography rules. He wanted exactly what the future of learning has now become—focused, practical, modular skills.

"Teach me the quick things," he insisted.

"How to type fast."

"How to make a text-heavy newspaper ad in fifteen minutes."

"How to correct twenty pages of copy errors without messing anything up."

And boy, did he learn. He absorbed the essentials with a kind of hunger you can't manufacture in classrooms. Within months, he was faster at production work than many junior trainees. Within a year, he convinced our general manager to help him buy a small second-hand computer. He set up a corner outside our AC cabin and began helping everyone with "odd jobs"—quick corrections, colour options for last-minute client changes, layout fixes, typesetting.

When I was transferred to another branch a few years later, I saw Babu one last time. He was no longer the boy serving chai or coffee. He was an indispensable part of the studio, earning a respectable salary, and more importantly, earning respect.

Looking back now, I realize:

Babu was living the future long before the future arrived.

He did not have a degree.

He did not have credentials.

He did not have English fluency or textbook theory.

But he had the three things the twenty-first century now demands from all of us: curiosity, courage and continuous learning.

He learned in bits and pieces—exactly the way nanodegrees work today. He learned after-hours—exactly the way modular learning fits into real lives. He learned what was *useful now*—not what might someday be relevant. Most importantly, he learned because he *wanted* to, not because anyone forced him.

And that is the heart of this chapter. The world no longer rewards the person who knows the most on Day One—it rewards the person who keeps learning on Day Thousand.

Babu taught me that the future of education is not in degrees; it is in momentum. It is not in certificates; it is in skill stacks. It is not in classrooms; it is in everyday curiosity—in canteens, corridors, lunch breaks and late-night studios.

When I think of the accelerating pace of AI today, I often think of that boy standing at the glass door, eyes full of wonder, refusing to wait for permission to learn.

The future will belong not to the most educated, but to the most *eager*. Not to the credentialed, but to the *curious*. Not to those who once learned, but to those who never stop.

DATA IS THE KEY—OWN IT, DECODE IT AND SHAPE THE FUTURE

Why Clarity Is More Valuable than Precision

We do not compete with machines. We evolve with them.

Studying our digital footprint as active learning tools

In the digital age, every person leaves behind a trail, which is made up of more than social media posts or online purchases. It is in how long we linger on a webpage, which emails we open first, what time our phone's alarm goes off, or which direction we scroll. Whether we realize it or not, we are a walking, talking data generator or an engine producing signals constantly. But here is the critical question: Are we the author of our own data story, or merely a character in someone else's plot?

Owning our data is no longer just a conversation about protecting our privacy or complying with laws. It is about recognizing our data for what it is: a high-value asset, deeply personal, profoundly predictive and uniquely powerful. Think of it as digital autobiography being written in real time. But this one is written by algorithms, sorted by strangers and often sold to advertisers before we ever see a word of it.

The difference between passively existing in a data world and actively engaging with it is the difference between being a product and being a person. Demis Hassabis and his work introduced reinforcement learning at DeepMind—a model where artificial agents learn by trial and error, adjusting behaviour based on past outcomes. Interestingly, humans often forget to apply the same principle to themselves. What if we examined our own digital footprints not only as passive histories, but as active learning tools?

We need to start simple. Use screen time apps not to shame ourselves, but to see patterns. Use location tracking tools to understand our habits, not just for convenience. Look at your weekly movement patterns—how often you visit certain places, how long you stay and how your routines cluster around specific times of day. You may notice, for instance, that all your "quick breaks" happen near junk-food outlets, or that you consistently avoid certain neighbourhoods without realizing it.

We can use health and fitness apps not only to hit a step count but to explore how our energy shifts with diet, sleep and stress. These are not merely productivity hacks; they are mechanisms of authorship. They are ways to read our own data and begin editing our behaviour.

Owning our data also means becoming aware of who else is using it. Are we giving consent for value in return or merely for convenience? When we sign into a website through a social account, when we let apps track us across platforms, when we agree to personalized recommendations, what are we trading? Most of the time, it is attention. And attention is currency. Because every click, scroll, pause and hesitation becomes a data signal that platforms can convert into advertising revenue, behavioural predictions and influence.

True ownership is not about withdrawing from digital life; it is about mastering it. We should think of our data not as a stream of numbers, but as a reflection of our character, our decisions, our struggles and our growth. The power lies in mining our own data before others do and learning more from it than they ever could. When we analyze our patterns, we not just interpreting numbers we are uncovering our intentions, blind spots and emotional triggers that no algorithm can fully understand. This transforms our data from something that predicts us into something that empowers us.

Professionals in the AI era must transition from being unaware participants in data ecosystems to becoming mindful narrators of their own data lives. Only then will they be able to reframe their data story—not as something being written about them, but something being written by them.

Because when we own our data, we also own the decisions that arise from it. We own the patterns that shape our behaviour. And ultimately, we own the future that data is helping design for us.

Understanding data with clarity

Data is alluring. It promises certainty, it offers graphs and metrics and it seduces professionals into believing that having data is the same as having insight. But let us be clear—data, by itself, is not wisdom. It is just potential. It is not reality—it is a representation of reality. And unless we learn to interpret it critically, we risk being misled by our own tools.

Fei-Fei Li's groundbreaking ImageNet project enabled machines to see. By effectively utilizing crowdsourcing, Li curated over millions of annotated images, which substantially improved the accuracy of image recognition algorithms. It worked because millions of human-labelled images taught the machines how to interpret what was in front of them. The real innovation was not just in feeding the machine data; it was in structuring that data with meaning. Clarity, not quantity, changed the game.

"The only path to build intelligent machines is to enable it with powerful visual intelligence, just like what animals did in evolution."

—Fei-Fei Li

Similarly, what separates data professionals from data-dependent professionals is clarity. We don't need more dashboards—we need better questions. Every metric we look at is a mirror reflecting back a worldview. But whose worldview? What is being emphasized and what is being overlooked? These are analytical questions as well as ethical ones.

When you see a 30 per cent increase in user engagement, do you celebrate? Maybe. But first, ask: What does engagement mean in this context? Is it healthy usage or addictive behaviour? When you observe a drop in employee productivity on a time-tracking tool, is it burnout or just a shift in priorities? Without deeper questioning, even accurate data can drive poor decisions. There can be an argument—this has always been the case with data. It is dependent on human interpretation. What is different about AI data?

The difference is its scale and speed—its patterns influence decisions automatically and continuously, often long before anyone has the chance to interpret or question them.

Clarity requires us to slow down. We must resist the pressure to act on every chart and instead create space for thoughtful interpretation. These days, data literacy must go beyond skills in Excel or Python. It must include philosophical literacy. Understanding that all numbers come with built-in assumptions. That every dataset is partial. That silence in data—the missing voices, the excluded groups—can be as informative as the figures we do see.

Professionals often fall into the trap of "false precision". We get excited by numbers like 89.4 per cent satisfaction, but overlook the fact that the survey had a low response rate, or that it excluded certain regions. What looks like confidence is sometimes just convenience. Real intelligence begins when we ask what is missing, not merely what is present.

And here is the paradox: The more data we have, the more interpretation matters. More metrics do not make us more objective. In fact, the more data we collect, the more we are at risk of becoming biased if we are not intentional about how we analyze it. Data gives us patterns; it is our job to give them meaning.

There is another danger too: using data to validate rather than challenge. It is easy to cherry-pick stats to reinforce pre-existing narratives. That is not intelligence; that is marketing. True intelligence asks, "What would disprove my assumption?" "What data might I be ignoring because it makes me uncomfortable?"

To lead with data is not to drown in it. It is to navigate through it, knowing that we are the one steering the ship, not the one being swept along by the tide. Data can illuminate. But clarity is what lets us see.

In a noisy world, clarity is power. It doesn't come from having more data. It comes from having more insight. And insight only emerges when we apply critical thinking, practice ethical reflection, and, above all, have the courage to say, "Let's slow down and understand what this really means."

Because data, like all language, is never neutral. It speaks, and it matters how we choose to listen.

Weaponizing insight responsibly

If owning data is about awareness and understanding it is about clarity, then weaponizing it is about action. But not all actions are ethical. Not every use of data is beneficial.

To weaponize (or manipulate) data means to use it with accuracy. It means using our insights to negotiate better contracts, to time our market moves more smartly, to personalize our services with empathy. It does not imply exploiting ignorance. The line between strategy and manipulation is thin, but it matters.

Look at how companies use A/B testing to optimize websites. A small change in the colour of a button or a word can drive sales. That is weaponization (or manipulation). But it can also be deployed to trap users in dark patterns, nudging them towards decisions they did not intend to make.

Fei-Fei Li often emphasizes that AI should be designed with human values in mind. The same must apply to how we use personal and organizational data. The question is not just "What can I do with this information?" but also "What *should* I do?"

Data weaponization without ethics leads to mistrust. When data is used carelessly or manipulatively, it breeds mistrust. But when it is handled with transparency and ethical intention, it becomes a powerful differentiator. It allows us to anticipate needs before they are expressed, reduce inefficiency and lead with insight instead of instinct.

The best experts will not be those who have access to the most data. It will be those who know how to convert small insights into big advantages without crossing the ethical line.

Building a personal data strategy

What if we approached our own life like a prototype? What if we treated our routines, habits and patterns with the same curiosity and rigour a startup brings to early user data? That is the heart of building a personal data strategy—not to quantify our existence, but to evolve it.

Most professionals touch their personal data only at the surface. They skim their sleep scores, check weekly screen time reports, glance at performance reviews and move on. The real transformation begins when we stop treating data as a side note and start treating it as a tool for intentional change.

We need to start with a radical shift in our mindset: we are our most important project.

Every action we take emits data—tiny signals about how we spend our time, where our energy dips, when we feel most focused and which environments make us thrive. This data isn't for machines to harvest; it is for us to harness. What you track, you can question. What you question, you can improve.

We need to build a dashboard for our life. Not a sterile spreadsheet, but a personal cockpit—an interface that shows us how we are living. We need to use wearable tech or analog journals. Try tools like mood trackers, digital planners, sleep monitors like Oura or Fitbit, habit apps like Streaks, bullet journals that reveal patterns in our day, even browser extensions that reflect how we spend our time online. A weekly glance at these tools can show us when we are energised, when we are overloaded and where our time is quietly disappearing. Layer in qualitative reflections with the quantitative stuff. Numbers tell us *what* is happening. Only we can tell *why*.

We need to think in experiments. What happens when we wake up without screens for a week? What patterns emerge if we delay checking email until noon? These are not lifestyle fads. They are micro-experiments with measurable outputs. Treat each one as a feedback loop—observe, adjust, reflect, repeat.

Importantly, this is not about surveillance; it is about authorship. We are not collecting data to punish or optimize ourselves like a machine. We are collecting it to identify our patterns and our triggers and align our days with our values. We are designing a better version of ourselves with data as our mirror, not our master.

The future-ready professional is not just skilful; they are self-aware. Growth is no longer a mystery or a gift of luck. It is a deliberate, designed outcome shaped by insight, curiosity and the courage to iterate on our own life.

Embedding ethics and intelligence in organizational data cultures

While individual data strategy matters, organizational cultures determine scale. A company that treats data only as a KPI factory will miss the deeper potential. But one that cultivates data ethics and storytelling can become truly transformative.

What does a healthy data culture look like?

First, it values transparency. Metrics aren't just shared upwards with executives; they are shared laterally and with context.

Second, it facilitates interpretation. People are trained not just to use dashboards, but to ask insightful questions about what the numbers mean.

Third, it values diverse perspectives. The most dangerous decisions in data-driven teams come from monocultures. Confirmation bias takes root when everyone interprets the same signal the same way. But when teams are interdisciplinary—engineers, designers, ethicists—they create richer insights.

And lastly, a smart data culture builds in friction. Yes, friction. Not every decision should be automated or optimized. Sometimes, slowing down to reflect is the most ethical act.

Hassabis reminds us that intelligence is not speed; it is depth. The same applies to data strategy.

Organizations must design rituals for data storytelling. Three things should be included with every dataset: the context of its collection, the underlying assumptions it rests on and the voices it may leave out. After all, as Hassabis puts it, "It is in this collaboration between people and algorithms that incredible scientific progress lies over the next few decades."

Consider a public-health NGO analyzing maternal health data across rural districts. If the team simply looks at the numbers—clinic visits, anaemia levels, institutional deliveries—they might design the wrong intervention. But when they include the *context* (seasonal migration, flooded roads, cultural norms), recognize the *assumptions* (that women can travel freely, that clinics are functional), and identify the *missing voices* (women who never reach the health system at all), the dataset transforms. Suddenly, they understand why clinic footfall drops every monsoon, why anaemia persists despite supplements, why frontline workers struggle.

When these elements are honoured, data becomes more than numbers. It becomes wisdom, which is the foundation for interventions that actually work.

Data literacy is the new power divide

In earlier times, the divide between power and poverty was often about land, money or weapons. Today, it is increasingly about data literacy. If we look back through history, we will find empires rose and fell on the back of land, wealth or firepower. But in the 21st century, power is being redefined and redistributed through the lens of data. But not just who owns it. Who understands it. Who can wield it with wisdom, creativity and responsibility.

Today's emerging divide is not just economic or technological. It is a literacy divide—a gap between those who are data-fluent and those who are data-blind.

However, data fluency is not the same as technical proficiency. It is not about knowing how to write code or build a dashboard. It is about knowing how to ask the right questions. For example, what is missing from this chart? Who decided what to measure? What assumptions are baked into this "objective" model? Why was this outlier excluded?

The new data elite are not buried in spreadsheets. They are in the boardroom, in policy discussions, in classrooms translating complexity into action. They don't just decode numbers; they tell stories with them. They ask: How can this insight lead to change? And for whom?

Fei-Fei Li's reminder is prescient: "The future belongs to those who can marry data with human empathy." In practice, this means blending two literacies—the ability to read datasets and the ability to read social dynamics. To spot the bias in a trend line. To hear the silence in a pie chart.

For example, take school performance data. A dashboard may show that one school consistently scores lower than others in the district. A purely data-driven reading might conclude that the teachers are underperforming or the students are less capable. But an empathetic reading asks different questions: Is this the only school where most children walk five kilometres to attend class? Is it serving first-generation learners? Are students juggling household responsibilities?

The trend line shows a gap; empathy reveals the *reasons* behind it. Without that second literacy, the data risks reinforcing stereotypes rather than solving the problem. To know that every statistical output has a social input, and often, a historical injustice baked into it.

This chapter is not asking you to become a data scientist. It is urging you to become a data citizen—someone who can engage with data as both a source of truth and a source of power. Someone who knows that behind every algorithm are human decisions, and behind every visualization is a worldview.

Data literacy is the new civic duty, not just "a nice to have". It impacts how we comprehend health policies, climate change forecasts, AI-powered platforms, or even the personalization of our newsfeed. In a world increasingly governed by models and metrics, how we interpret and challenge those systems becomes an expression of our agency.

The ability to read, question and speak data may just be the defining skill of our time.

How I learned it

Long before I ever wrote about data as a mirror, a narrative, a feedback loop, I was living inside those loops without realizing it. My relationship with data did not begin with dashboards or apps—it began with tiny experiments I ran on myself, long before the language of "behavioural insights" and "reinforcement learning" became fashionable. Over time, I discovered that the simplest shifts in routine often revealed the deepest truths about who I was becoming.

One of the most transformative experiments I ever tried was deceptively small: I stopped looking at screens for the first hour of my morning. I did not do it for productivity. I did it out of curiosity. Within a week, my mind began to settle into a kind of morning clarity I had never experienced before. Ideas that used to arrive scattered now lined up in order. My writing gained depth. My emotions gained space. Only later did I realize what had happened: I was not avoiding technology—I was observing myself. I was reading my own behavioural data in real time.

Another experiment followed years later: delaying email until noon. It felt reckless at first, almost like breaking a rule of adulthood.

But what emerged was a profound insight into my cognitive rhythm. My best thinking hours—the quiet mornings—were no longer fragmented by responsive tasks. I could see the pattern clearly: administrative work was hijacking the same emotional bandwidth that creative work needed. My data was not in a spreadsheet; it was in the shift I felt in my body, my focus, my energy. And once I saw the pattern, I could not unsee it.

Even my habit of longhand journaling at night taught me more than any analytics dashboard. I noticed how emotional spikes correlated with poor sleep, how difficult conversations left traces in my mood the next day, how travel revitalized me even when it exhausted me physically. These observations were not just reflections—they were iterations, small adjustments shaping the next day's choices. Hassabis calls this "learning from reward signals". I call it listening to myself.

Over time, I understood what this chapter argues: Data is not the numbers outside you. It is the patterns inside you. And unless you learn to read those patterns consciously, someone else will read them for you—algorithms, platforms, advertisers, systems that do not always have your well-being at heart.

These personal experiments also taught me the subtle art of interpretation. Just like AI systems, humans generate data constantly, but its meaning is never obvious. A spike in screen time could mean boredom, burnout or creativity. A dip in productivity could signal disengagement or simply a shift in priorities. Data does not speak; we speak through it. And like Harari reminds us, the story we tell is shaped by our history, our biases, our fears. Learning to interpret my own behavioural signals with humility became one of the most important skills I ever developed.

Gradually, I also learned how to leverage what I observed. Not as manipulation, but as alignment. When I noticed that certain environments made me more imaginative, I designed more of my day around them. When I saw that specific triggers drained me emotionally, I restructured my schedule. When I found that certain kinds of discomfort made me grow, I leaned into them deliberately. I wasn't optimizing myself for productivity. I was optimizing myself for clarity.

These years of micro-experiments—tiny acts of noticing, adjusting, repeating—became my personal dashboard long before wearable tech made dashboards fashionable. They showed me what this chapter insists on: data literacy is not about coding; it is about consciousness. It is about treating your life like a living system—one you test, refine and evolve with intention.

Looking back, I realize that everything I learned about adaptive behaviour, self-reflection, ethical restraint and iterative improvement came not from a classroom but from observing myself as carefully as a scientist observes an experiment. That is why I believe the divide today is not between those who can analyze data and those who cannot—it is between those who question their data and those who accept it blindly.

In a world where data is the currency of choice, the greatest power we hold is the ability to see—not just what the numbers say, but what they reveal about the story we are authoring every day. And perhaps the most important lesson of all is that the more consciously we read our data, the more intentionally we can rewrite our life.

SKILLS THAT EVEN SUPERINTELLIGENCE CAN'T REPLICATE

What Gives Us Our Competitive Advantage

To thrive in a machine-shaped world, we must deepen the qualities that make us uniquely human—our passion, stories, empathy and judgement.

In a world increasingly defined by machine intelligence, many of us have begun to wonder: What remains uniquely human?

During an hour-long public conversation with Senator Bernie Sanders at Georgetown University in November 2025, Geoffrey

Hinton has said it wouldn't be "inconceivable" that humankind gets wiped out by AI. He also believes we are not that far away from achieving an artificial general intelligence, or AGI, a hypothetical AI system with human or superhuman levels of intelligence that is able to perform a vast array of tasks, which the AI industry is obsessed with building.

"Until quite recently, I thought it was going to be like 20 to 50 years before we have general purpose AI," Hinton said in 2023. "And now I think it may be 20 years or less."

Strikingly, Hinton now claims that the latest models like OpenAI's GPT-5 "know thousands of times more than us already."

Yet even in this shifting landscape, there are elements of the human spirit that machines cannot imitate. These qualities are not stored in silicon or expressed in code; they are carved in consciousness and shaped by experience. This chapter explores four such irreplaceable traits: passion, storytelling, emotional intelligence and judgement. One may ask, What about vision, intuition or imagination? The truth is, these four traits form the foundations from which vision emerges. Vision is not a standalone gift—it is the synthesis of passion, the narrative power of storytelling, the sensitivity of emotional intelligence and the discernment of judgement. That is why we spotlight these pillars: they are the engines that make every higher human capacity possible.

As machines become faster, more accurate and eerily predictive, our edge as human beings will depend on cultivating what algorithms lack: the heart, the messiness, the contradiction and the deeper meaning. Sherry Turkle, one of the most respected thinkers on human–technology relationships, reminds us 'Technology proposes itself as the architect of our intimacies. But if we do not cultivate our own inner lives, we risk outsourcing the very things that make us human.'

If we want to survive and thrive in a world dominated by artificial minds, we must begin not by competing with them, but by deepening the gifts they cannot possess.

Passion—the irreplaceable drive

Passion is irrational. And that is precisely what makes it so powerful.

Algorithms do not dream. They don't suffer sleepless nights thinking about a breakthrough that does not yet exist. They don't feel euphoria when a solution arrives after days of confusion. Humans do. And that is where our enduring advantage lies.

The great achievements in history were not born from efficiency—they were born from obsession. Marie Curie did not isolate radium because it was the most rational use of her time. She did it because something inside her refused to give up. Steve Jobs did not revolutionize technology because a spreadsheet told him to. He did it because he *felt* it had to be done. That feeling—illogical, inconvenient and often exhausting—is passion.

Passion is not a luxury but a necessity more so in the workplace. Passion does not just adorn our work; it animates it. It is the voice that says, "There must be a better way", even when everyone else is satisfied. It is the desire to pay attention to the details that others dismiss. It is the difference between adequate and remarkable.

Artificial intelligence is designed to maximize objectives within boundaries. Passion, however, creates new boundaries. It does not just optimize the game; it reinvents it. That is a fundamentally human act. A machine will never sit by a campfire and write a poem that changes lives. It will never go into debt to fund a dream. But people do—again and again—because we are wired not just for survival, but for significance.

Yes, user prompts, allowing for various styles and themes, have generated so-called poems in the past but they are not worthy of discussion.

And significance often starts with discomfort. Passion is not always comfortable or clean. It is not a neat line on a Gantt chart. It is chaotic, stubborn, emotional. And it leads to failure frequently. But passion transforms failure into resilience. It teaches us to see each setback as a signal, not a stop sign. That is something AI still can't understand. It doesn't *feel* the lesson in loss. But we do. And feeling the sting of loss is what rewires us—it forces reflection, deepens commitment and builds the inner strength that keeps us moving when logic alone would tell us to stop.

In corporate environments increasingly enamoured with dashboards and KPIs, passion is sometimes seen as a wildcard—too volatile and inconsistent. But its role is misunderstood. Passion is not the opposite of logic; it is the ignition of logic. It gives us the *why* before we build the *how*. When people are passionate, metrics follow, not the other way around.

There is also a deeper societal challenge at play. In an AI-dominated era, there is a risk we devalue what can't be measured. But the most meaningful things in life are inherently immeasurable—love, courage, justice, hope. Passion lives in that same space. We must learn to defend its place in our systems, not because it is effective, but because it is human.

Demis Hassabis may have taught machines how to learn from reward loops, but humans chase things even when there is no reward in sight. That irrational pursuit is how breakthroughs happen. It is what makes scientists keep working through experiments that fail ninety-nine times out of hundred. Thomas A. Edison's famous quote, "I have not failed. I have just found 10,000 ways that won't work," encapsulates the resilient spirit of one of history's greatest inventors. It is what causes artists throw out a finished piece because it does not "feel" right. While AI can analyze, passion dares.

To be human is to want something more than output. It is to feel pulled towards meaning, purpose or even mystery. That is not inefficiency; it is excellence in its most sacred form.

So, in the face of rising AI, the most strategic thing we can do is not suppress passion to fit into systems but protect it, amplify it and lead with it. Because in a world increasingly run by code, the fire in the human heart is no longer just important; it is irreplaceable.

Storytelling—architecture of meaningful connection

Facts don't change minds; stories do.

In a world teeming with data, storytelling is not optional it is essential. We often think of stories as entertainment or as tools for marketing. But in truth, storytelling is the ancient architecture of human understanding. It is how we remember; it is how we care; it is how we decide what matters.

A chart can show us that poverty is declining. But only a story can help us *feel* what that means for a mother in a remote village who no longer skips meals to feed her children. That emotional connection is the bridge between knowledge and action. It is a bridge machines cannot yet walk on.

Artificial intelligence can certainly generate text. It can even imitate style, tone, rhythm, but it does not understand the heartbreak behind a single word choice. It does not ache for a character's redemption. It does not struggle with which memory to reveal and which one to keep hidden. Because true storytelling is not just words; it is wisdom, feeling, timing and human intuition.

When Yuval Harari talks about sapiens as "the storytelling animal", he is pointing to our unique evolutionary gift. It is not just language that set us apart; it is narrative. Stories helped early humans collaborate, create culture and build civilization. Today, they help us navigate complexity. In a world flooded with information, stories filter signal from noise. They help us prioritize. They help us care. They drive cultural change, uplift diverse voices and fosters deeper human connection.

Leaders who understand this don't just present ideas; they frame them. They don't just report results; they tell the story of the journey. Think of Barack Obama's speeches, especially during the first election campaign or Greta Thunberg's blunt appeals. Obama used storytelling as a tool for inclusion and representation. They move people not through data, but through narrative resonance. The listener doesn't just understand; they *feel seen*.

The following real-world AI-generated story examples illustrate some of those limitations:

- The first short film scripted entirely by AI in 2016, *Sunspring,* is baffling and odd when processed by a rational, emotional human. One could have argued at the time that AI would never replace humans for script writing.
- *The Safe Zone* was written and directed by AI. It is more refined than *Sunspring* but still a bit clunky.

The storytelling community wrestles with two big questions when it comes to AI:

1. Can humans and AI come together to create and tell better stories?

2. Is there a perfect balance between how much of a story is derived from the human brain versus what is augmented by AI?

The answer may be a matter of perspective. Aaron Kemmer, who co-produced *The Safe Zone*, said, "I could easily see AI leading to personalized movies…where you can see any variation of any film you've ever wanted. Watch Tom Cruise play as Iron Man battling Darth Vader…or an infinite number (of) ideas."

This power is not limited to politics or art. In business, storytelling is what turns a product into a movement. It is what turns a brand into a belief system. It is what makes your idea stick when competitors are offering similar features. Because humans do not buy logic; they buy emotion wrapped in logic. This power is not limited to politics or art. In business, storytelling is what turns a product into a movement. It is what transforms a brand into a belief system—something people don't just buy, but identify with. And I saw this play out firsthand in the late nineties when we introduced KitKat chocolate bar in an Indian market already dominated by Cadbury and Amul chocolates. Logically, there was no space for another chocolate bar. But we were not selling a chocolate. We were selling a *moment*. The line "Have a Break, Have a KitKat" did not describe the product; it described a human need. In a culture where snacks, sweets and chocolates were shared more than savoured privately, "the break" became a socially loaded idea—an emotional shorthand for pausing, sharing, resetting, breathing.

What made the campaign powerful was not the wafer or the flavour it was the behavioural truth we tapped into. Everyone needs a break—students, office workers, homemakers, families. The product became a ritual, not a treat. KitKat was not competing on taste; it was competing on meaning. That is the power of narrative: it attaches a human behaviour to an object and elevates it from a commodity to a companion. Competitors could copy the features, but they could not copy the *feeling*. And this is why storytelling remains irreplaceably human because it is built not from code, but from culture, emotion and lived experience.

Storytelling also helps us confront uncertainty. When the world feels chaotic, people don't want more numbers—they want meaning. They want to hear a voice that says, "Here's what it means, here's where we've been, here's where we might go." That is not manipulation; it is guidance.

Even in data-driven domains, story matters. A health report can list statistics on disease prevalence. But unless that data is framed in human terms—who is affected, why it matters, what can be done— it fails to inspire action. Storytelling is the amplifier that makes data resonate.

Don't you think, as AI gets better at producing language, human storytelling becomes more valuable, not less?

Because in a world where machines can generate infinite content, it is meaning that becomes scarce. And only humans, *for now*, can tell stories that carry deep, authentic, emotional truth.

So, we must teach storytelling not just to writers or marketers, but to engineers, data scientists, doctors and diplomats. Everyone who interacts with information must learn how to shape meaning.

Not to embellish facts, but to honour them, to guide interpretation, invite reflection and build shared understanding.

As we rush to optimize, automate and streamline, we must not forget that the greatest human influence does not come from systems. It comes from stories. And those who master them will shape not just conversations but the future. Storytelling is more than entertainment—it is a vehicle for hope, inclusion and pluralism. Stories can inspire people to imagine and work towards a more just and inclusive society.

However, Stephen Hawking cautions, "The development of full artificial intelligence could spell the end of the human race. Once humans develop artificial intelligence, it will take off on its own, and redesign itself at an ever-increasing rate." His warning captures the existential anxiety that accompanies every major technological leap.

But it is equally important to hold space for a more optimistic view. As Fei-Fei Li argues, "AI is not a replacement for human intelligence; it is an extension of it." Similarly, Hassabis notes that the true promise of AI lies in solving problems too complex for humans alone. These perspectives remind us that the future of AI is not predetermined doom but a spectrum of possibilities—shaped by how thoughtfully, ethically and imaginatively we build it.

Emotional intelligence—empathy that connects

Artificial intelligence does not feel awkward. It does not wince when it says the wrong thing. It does not understand the weight of silence in a room.

That is emotional intelligence which the machines don't have.

Popularized by psychologist Daniel Goleman, emotional intelligence is the ability to recognize, understand and manage one's own emotions while navigating those of others. Goleman highlighted emotional intelligence's role in leadership, conflict resolution and empathy-driven decision-making, emphasizing its relevance across settings—from corporate boardrooms to family dinners.

We live in a social world. Careers are built on trust, teams thrive on empathy and leadership requires nuance. Emotional quotient is more predictive of success in many fields than IQ. Why? Because humans are not logic machines. We are mood-driven, experience-shaped context-sensitive beings.

When a colleague walks into a room with slumped shoulders and avoids eye contact, you pick up on it. You ask, you adapt. An AI assistant might continue with the calendar.

Emotional intelligence is about reading between the lines, sensing unspoken cues and knowing when *not* to say something. It is about timing, tone, presence.

As machines get better at everything else, it is our emotional intelligence that will distinguish us.

In high-stakes negotiations, in crisis management, in teaching, parenting, caregiving emotional intelligence is irreplaceable. These are not just social niceties; they are human lifelines.

Emotional intelligence can be nurtured. It grows with reflection, feedback and compassion. In a future where many technical skills are outsourced to machines, emotional intelligence may become the most valuable leadership currency.

Imagine a manager who can read the energy of a room, sense fear or fatigue and change course. That is not in the playbook of artificial intelligence. That is a human instinct, that is human superpower.

The AI era calls for not more humanity, not less. To thrive, we must elevate the social and emotional dimensions of our work because empathy will never be a plug-in.

But AI is quickly evolving to recognize and respond to human emotions with increased efficiency—a field known as affective computing. Coined by MIT professor Rosalind Picard in the 1990s, affective computing is a field at the intersection of computer science, psychology, neuroscience and cognitive science. The goal is to bridge the emotional gap between humans and machines, enabling more natural and empathetic interactions. Humanoid robots, machines designed to mimic human appearance and behaviour are becoming increasingly powerful with integration of affective computing.

Judgement—compass in complexity

Artificial intelligence is rapidly reshaping the legal field. Tools now assist in legal research, predict case outcomes, draft contracts and even generate preliminary judgements in routine matters. For countries like India, where judicial delays cripple the system, the possibility of AI reducing pendency is undeniably appealing.

China offers an early glimpse of this future. Some courts now use generative AI to analyze evidence and propose rulings for low-complexity cases—always reviewed by human judges, but increasingly influential in the decision chain. This brings both promise and caution. Artificial intelligence can speed up routine processes, but justice is not just efficiency; it requires context, empathy and moral reasoning.

The real question is not whether AI should enter the courtroom, but how far and under whose judgement it should go.

Data is abundant, but judgement is rare.

Artificial intelligence can process a billion parameters in seconds, but it lacks discernment. It does not weigh ethics, context or long-term impact. Judgement does.

Judgement is not the same as intelligence; it is deeper. It integrates knowledge, values, consequences and timing. It understands when to act and when to wait, when to follow rules and when to break them.

Imagine a self-driving car that must decide between two tragic outcomes in a crash. Should the passengers in the vehicle be sacrificed to save pedestrians? Or should a pedestrian be killed to save a family of four in the vehicle? The data may offer options, but judgement asks: What is fair, what is right, what is just?

Judgement is forged over time. It is developed through mistakes, reflection and moral struggle. It requires experience—something machines do not accumulate the way humans do. Algorithms optimize for outcomes; humans wrestle with consequences.

A striking illustration comes from an MIT global study on autonomous vehicle ethics. Researchers found consistent worldwide preferences: people want cars to save humans over animals, protect the many over the few and favour the young over the old. But beneath this apparent consensus lay sharp regional differences shaped by culture, economics, religion and social norms. What one society sees as moral priority, another sees as moral compromise. These findings expose a deeper truth: even when presented with the same dilemma, human communities disagree on what "the right decision" looks like.

This is precisely where machines fall short. An AI can calculate probability, but it cannot navigate the cultural, emotional and moral weight behind those decisions. A self-driving car may be able to identify the safest manoeuvre, but it cannot understand the ethical pain embedded in choosing between two lives. Judgement is not pattern recognition; it is moral reasoning grounded in lived experience. And that remains a profoundly human domain.

Our greatest achievements and failures stem not from intelligence alone, but from our choices. Atomic bombs and civil rights movements both emerged from judgement calls.

In leadership, judgement is everything. Leaders must balance profit with purpose, speed with safety, innovation with responsibility. Artificial intelligence can suggest scenarios; only humans can weigh their worth.

Judgement also includes the courage to say, "I don't know". Artificial intelligence rarely says that. It offers outputs regardless of confidence, but humans can choose humility, which can save lives.

Developing judgement requires wide exposure to literature, ethics and history. It grows in ambiguity, not clarity. That is why the liberal arts remain crucial even in a tech-driven world.

To lead in the age of AI is to become more human, not less. Judgement is the inner compass that keeps us true.

"Even a cat has things it can do that AI cannot."

—Fei-Fei Li

How I learned it

I did not begin my career as a storyteller. Far from it. As I mentioned earlier, I only trained myself to write advertising headlines, subheads and the occasional few lines of copy—sharp, functional fragments designed to sell a product or shape a perception. Storytelling, in the deeper, human sense of the word, belonged to novelists, poets, filmmakers. Not to me.

And then, one ordinary morning on my way to the office, I saw Rehman.

He was a tiny boy—eight years old maybe—standing at a traffic signal in South Delhi where I stopped every day. Some days he begged; some days he simply observed the world with an intensity uncommon even among adults. There was an alertness in him, an intelligence that flickered like a live wire. Slowly, almost imperceptibly, we became friends.

One day he declared, with the pride of a seasoned entrepreneur, "*Main ab bhikhari nahin raha. Main businessman ban gaya* (I am no longer a beggar; I am a businessman now)."

I laughed and asked him what business he ran. And he replied, with absolute clarity, "*Kai saare. Kabhi magazine bechta hoon, kabhi phool, toh kabhi tiranga* (I have many products to sell; sometimes I sell magazines; sometimes I sell flowers; sometimes our national flag)." He wasn't talking about survival. He was talking about possibilities.

That afternoon, I went to the office and actually could do nothing. The creative briefs on my desk went unread. The layouts stayed untouched. Something inside me had shifted. Rehman's eyes held a dream too large for my regular advertising vocabulary to contain. That day, instinctively, I reached for something deeper within myself—something I had not known I possessed.

I wrote a song: "A Song for Rehman". It was not planned. It was not polished. It was not even something I intended to show anyone. But it came from a place where passion met empathy, where storytelling emerged from witnessing another human being with complete presence, where judgement helped me decide what truth must be told.

That one song after I composed and sang it travelled farther than anything I had written before. It received international recognition, awards, invitations from European universities and for nearly a decade became a tool for fundraising across many music platforms—supporting NGOs, touching lives far beyond that South Delhi signal. And today, long after the spotlight has dimmed, it continues to live quietly on its original portal:

https://www.reverbnation.com/victorghoshe

Looking back, I realize this: that day, Rehman unlocked in me the four irreplaceable human capacities we have just discussed in this chapter—passion, storytelling, emotional intelligence and judgement. Not through a workshop. Not through a course. But through presence. Through empathy. And through the courage to feel something and transform it into expression.

Artificial intelligence can analyze a child's face, classify his expression, even generate a technically perfect song about him, but it cannot *feel* the moment that moved me. It cannot experience the jolt of human connection that rearranges your inner landscape. It cannot be transformed by another person's dream.

And this is why these traits remain our deepest advantage.

They are not competencies.

They are catalysts.

They turn strangers into stories, suffering into art and fleeting encounters into lifelong meaning.

Rehman did not just inspire a song. He taught me the very lesson this chapter is trying to impart: we outlive machines not by thinking faster, but by feeling deeper. Because what remains when machines can do almost everything is the one thing they cannot touch—the human core that turns a traffic signal into a revelation and a child's dream into a story the world can feel.

THE RISE OF OUR DIGITAL TWIN

How Our Digital Mirrors Will Shape Our Habits, Identity and Growth

The more consciously we engage with our data, the more deliberately we can shape our future.

The birth of the digital twin

For as long as human beings have existed, we have searched for reflections of ourselves. We carved our likeness into cave walls, painted portraits on stone, molded statues from clay and bronze, and eventually captured our faces in photographs and films. But today, something altogether different is happening: our reflection is no longer frozen in image. It breathes in lines of code, learns from patterns, adapts and speaks back to us. This reflection is not of flesh and blood but of algorithms and data. It is the concept of the digital twin—a copy of humanity not made of cells but of silicon, not written in DNA but in binary code.

The idea of a digital twin is not science fiction. Already, industries use digital twins of machines, factories, and even cities to simulate and predict real-world behaviour. But what if AI could extend this to people? Could it become humanity's digital twin—a parallel self that thinks, remembers and acts as a reflection of our minds?

The term "digital twin" emerged in engineering. Imagine building a new aircraft engine. Before constructing it in the physical world, engineers create a virtual copy—an exact digital simulation that responds to stress, airflow and temperature just as a real engine would. This digital twin allows problems to be identified before they happen, risks to be reduced, and improvements to be made without costly trial and error.

This idea has spread into medicine, where digital twins of hearts, lungs or entire immune systems can be simulated to test treatments before applying them to patients. It has expanded into urban planning, where cities are mirrored in virtual environments to optimize traffic, energy use and infrastructure.

But once we grasp the power of digital twinning for machines and systems, the question arises: Why stop there? If we can model a turbine or a city, could we not model a human being—not just our biology, but our personality, memories and consciousness?

What if there were a version of you that never slept, never forgot and never got distracted? A version that remembered every meeting, every conversation, every idea you ever had? That is not science fiction anymore. It is the emerging reality of the digital twin.

Inspired by Andrej Karpathy's work on neural nets and Demis Hassabis's deep dives into digital cognition, we find ourselves at the cusp of a new relationship between humans and machines. The digital twin is not just a replica; it is a cognitive partner. It is not built to replace your mind, but to extend it. It behaves like the mirror we never had—one that reflects back not just appearance, but possibility. At its core, a digital twin is a data-driven model of you. It learns from your behaviours, your decisions, your patterns. It observes how you respond under pressure, when you are creative, how you solve problems. In doing so, it becomes an ever-learning second self.

This second self can be your assistant, your editor, your strategist. It can remind you of how you have handled similar situations in the past, or simulate future outcomes based on your historical choices. Think of it as a coach that gets better with every interaction, a partner that matures as you grow.

But the implications stretch beyond productivity. With a digital twin, we start designing our lives, not just living them. The self becomes editable, improvable. We can experiment with new habits, simulate different choices and learn without risking real-world failure. It becomes a feedback loop of evolution, where our digital twin nudges us towards our potential self.

Of course, there are risks. The twin reflects not only our brilliance, but also our biases. If trained poorly, it can become an echo chamber of our worst habits. That is why this relationship must be conscious. We must engage with it not passively, but critically. Like any mirror, it can distort if not correctly framed.

Philosophically, the digital twin forces us to rethink identity. If my twin knows my preferences, my behaviours, my language—is it still me? Or something else entirely? Bill Gates might ask: How can this help us solve real problems?

The truth is, the digital twin is not just a tool; it is an invitation. To know ourselves more deeply; to work more intelligently; to live more deliberately. It is not about replacing humanity; it is about enhancing it. Treating AI as a competitor traps us in fear. Treating it as a coach unlocks possibility. And that change begins with mindset.

What does our digital twin sees that we don't

Everyone leaves a digital footprint. But today, we are not just talking about scattered breadcrumbs in the form of clicks, likes and transactions. We are talking about something deeper, quieter and far more intimate: a digital twin. Not a replica; not a sci-fi robot version of you; but a dynamic reflection of your preferences, your dislikes, your distractions, your joys.

This twin is built passively. We don't need to do anything special. Our Spotify playlist knows when we switch from jazz to techno at 11.30 p.m. Our Google calendar hints at when we say "yes" too often. Our smart watch detects a spike in heart rate every time we open emails from a certain someone. These are not trivial observations. They are layers. Layers that form the silhouette of your behaviour— often more honestly than you could articulate yourself.

Why does this matter?

Because for the first time in human history a version of you exists that is data-native—constructed not by memory or imagination, but by patterns. It sees the *you* that acts, not just the *you* that dreams. It tracks not your aspirations, but your choices.

The implications are philosophical and practical.

Philosophically, this twin challenges the traditional concept of identity. We have always believed in a story of self, shaped by reflections, dialogues and memories. But our digital twin has no story. It does not remember our excuses. It does not care about our intentions. It simply presents the sum of our actions. This can be both unsettling and liberating. Because when we see ourselves clearly, without narrative distortion, we can begin to *change*.

Practically, your digital twin acts like a cognitive fitness tracker—a steady companion measuring the rhythms of your day, highlighting what you might ignore.

Where does your time actually drain?

Which conversations do you avoid? What routines reliably spike your stress?

This is not accusation; it is awareness. And awareness is power.

Over time, these micro-insights help us break unhelpful habits, reinforce healthier ones and evolve in ways we rarely manage when left to intuition alone.

For half a century, scientists struggled to predict how proteins fold. A puzzle at the heart of understanding life and curing disease. Then, five years ago, the AlphaFold team cracked the code, which is one of biology's toughest puzzles. Hassabis and his team did not ask proteins, life's ingenious chemical tools, how they folded. They watched. They modeled. They learned by pattern. Life could not exist without proteins. That we can now predict protein structures and design our own proteins confer the greatest benefit to humankind. The profound scientific and societal value of this work was recognized in 2024 with the Nobel Prize in Chemistry.

Our digital twin does the same. We don't tell it who we are—it learns by observing. And sometimes, what it learns is uncomfortable.

But here is the crucial part: we don't have to be a passive subject in this process. By curating our digital habits, choosing the platforms we use, deciding how and when to engage, we start sculpting this mirror. We move from being observed to becoming the architect.

This also raises a profound question of control. Who owns this twin? Could corporations claim ownership of our twin because they collected our data? Who has access to it? If companies train algorithms based on our twins, they can predict our behaviours better than we can. Could governments use our twin to predict our behaviour or influence our choices? A digital twin could be weaponized—used for fraud, manipulation or identity theft. This is not paranoia; it is the modern condition. That is why digital literacy today must include self-awareness through data. It is not just about protecting our privacy. It is about protecting our autonomy.

Here is a simple start: run a screen-time report. Categorize your last hundred Google searches. Audit the apps you use between 10 p.m. and midnight. Observe without judgement. What you find will tell you more about your current state of mind than most self-help books.

Because this mirror does not reflect our face; it reflects our habits; it reflects our truth. And in a world increasingly shaped by AI, being able to meet our digital self—honestly, consciously and courageously—might just be the most human thing we can do.

Designing our AI-augmented routine

To understand how to integrate AI into our lives in a way that elevates, rather than dilutes, our humanity, we must ask a core question: How do we want to spend our time, energy and attention?

Artificial intelligence can do many things. But how to use it and when not to use it is a human choice.

Let us begin with daily decision-making. The average person makes hundreds of micro-decisions each day—what to read, whom to respond to, which events to attend. Artificial intelligence can help us triage and prioritize. Email assistants like Gmail's Smart Reply or scheduling tools like Clockwise are not just conveniences—they are the building blocks of our AI-augmented day.

Let us not stop there. Let us go deeper. Create an AI co-pilot that learns our patterns, anticipates our needs and nudges us towards focus. Use tools like Reclaim AI or Motion to align our calendar with our goals. Let ChatGPT help create meal plans. Let Grammarly sharpen our tone. Let AI transcription capture meetings so we can listen more and type less.

However, we must be cautious not to become passive recipients of automation. Our digital twin must reflect us, not *replace* us. This means periodically reviewing what our tools are doing on our behalf. Ask: Are they freeing me up for deeper thinking, or merely automating my distractions?

Designing our routine with AI requires intentionality. We could begin by mapping out our peak cognitive hours. Block those for tasks requiring human judgement, creativity or empathy. Then, outsource the rest. Let AI handle the repetitive, the sortable, the filterable.

The danger is not that AI will overtake us. The danger is that we might forget our own strengths while leaning on its crutches. We have to use it like a tool, not a crutch. That is why our AI-augmented routine must also include digital hygiene with built-in tech-free windows, mindfulness prompts and analog rituals.

In the end, our routine is our rhythm. Artificial intelligence can serve as your metronome, but you must write the music. That is the art of being augmented—not just efficient, but intentional.

The ethics of the digital

With power comes responsibility and no tool reflects this truth more sharply than AI. The digital twin we build will inevitably reflect our biases, limitations and values. The question is: Are they ours, or have they been inherited invisibly from the system?

If we feed your AI assistant biased data, it will amplify those biases. If your personal finance app learns from years of impulsive spending and distorted priorities, it may begin recommending short-term gratification over long-term stability—reinforcing the very habits you are trying to break. Ethics therefore is not an add-on—it is embedded in every input, prompt and dataset.

Here is a starting point: transparency. Do we know what data our AI tools are using? Do we know how decisions are made? The closer AI gets to our daily decisions, the more vital it becomes to audit its reasoning. Just like we expect explainability in leaders, we must demand it from algorithms.

Next comes consent. Are our colleagues aware that our meeting minutes are AI-transcribed? Are our clients comfortable with AI-generated reports? These are not just legal considerations; they are cultural and relational ones. When people don't know how their words or data are being captured, processed or reused, it can erode trust and create a sense of surveillance rather than collaboration.

Then there is ownership. If our digital twin becomes an archive of our insights, habits and intellectual property who owns it? What happens if the platform folds? These questions may seem technical, but they cut to the heart of autonomy.

But with these transformations come risks of disconnection. If people begin to rely more on digital twins than real human interaction, could we lose something essential about the texture of authentic relationships? Would grief, love and memory change if the digital self never truly dies?

Ethics in AI is not about fear; it is about foresight. Ethics is not a firewall; it is the DNA of our digital systems. We must remain vigilant about transparency, consent and control. We must proactively design our tools with human dignity, equity and sustainability in mind. Because once our digital becomes smart, it does not just reflect who we are; it influences who we become.

The digital twin is not just a technological possibility—it is a cultural and existential challenge. It asks us to redefine what it means to live, to die, to be remembered and to be human. If AI can replicate so much of us that it feels indistinguishable, what becomes of our uniqueness? Do we celebrate this as a triumph of technology, or fear it as the erosion of our humanity?

Crafting our digital wisdom loop

Imagine if every day we got just a little bit better—not just through experience, but through deliberate learning from our data. This is the promise of the wisdom loop: a cycle of action, reflection, feedback and improvement, powered by our AI companion.

Think of it like having a mentor that never sleeps. After our meetings, it highlights patterns—when we were most persuasive, or when tension spiked. After writing a strategy document, it compares our tone with past versions, flagging when we are drifting from our core message. After a product launch, it analyzes the signals from the market and offers refined insights. And on days when we are preparing for a big pitch, it even behaves like a brutally honest rehearsal partner—pointing out that we have used the phrase "game-changer" seven times, reminding us that our joke landed flat last time and suggesting a stronger opening line based on what has resonated before.

Tools like Notion AI, Mem and Roam Research are already helping users build second brains. The key is to go beyond passive note-taking. Build a system where our past insights are discoverable, linkable and evolvable. Where our digital self is not a static archive, but a living dialogue.

We can set rituals where every Friday, we review our week with AI support. We need to ourselves: What did I learn? What could I have done better? Where did I fall into patterns? Every month, we need to run retrospectives across our calendar and notes to spot blind spots or trends.

Over time, we create a flywheel of personal growth. The wisdom loop closes the gap between who we are and who we are becoming. But it requires humility—the willingness to be seen clearly, even by a machine.

The digital twin is not just about productivity; it is about consciousness; it is about evolving our operating system as a human. And like any system, its greatest strength lies not in code, but in continuous learning.

Reuniting the digital and the human

In our rush to digitize everything, we risk fragmenting ourselves. A task list here. A calendar there. A meditation app. A fitness tracker. A journal. But what is the thread that ties it all together? It is you.

The final and perhaps the most profound step in building an AI-augmented self is reunification. Let our digital systems speak to each other. But more importantly, let them all speak to us in a unified voice. Let our insights from work inform our wellness choices. Let our family calendar remind us of what truly matters during a hectic quarter. Let our values be visible in our productivity stack.

This requires intentional design. Begin by curating our ecosystem—not every app belongs; not every automation is helpful. We need to ask ourselves, "Does this make me more whole or more fragmented?"

Then create a dashboard of wholeness. Not just KPIs for our work, but a humane interface for our life. We need to include relationships, values, mood trends, health insights and creative goals. Let our digital twin remind us that we are not a machine but a meaning-making organism.

Finally, embed wonder. Not everything in life is measurable. We have to make space for awe, serendipity and silence. Teach our AI assistant not just our habits, but our hopes. At the same time, we need to remember that some dreams, doubts and inner battles must remain entirely human—AI should illuminate our path, not inherit our soul. Let it grow with us, not just track us.

We are not our apps. We are not our calendars. The digital twin must reflect the integrated self: mind, heart, body and spirit. When it does, it becomes a tool for self-actualization.

In the end, AI should not make us more efficient at being someone we are not. It should help us become more fully ourselves. Reuniting the digital and the human is not about balance; it is about harmony.

And harmony, unlike productivity, cannot be optimized. It must be lived.

The greatest power of AI is not in replacing us, but in helping us see ourselves more clearly. To build an AI-augmented self is not to become less human. It is to become a more conscious human. Just as a photograph is not the person but still carries their likeness, an AI twin may not be a soul but may nonetheless be a powerful representation.

But maybe the deeper truth is that the digital twin is not meant to replace us but to remind us. It reminds us of the beauty and fragility of our identity, of the responsibility that comes with technology, and of the eternal human desire to leave a mark beyond ourselves. In embracing this future, we must hold onto the humility that defines science itself: the understanding that even our most perfect reflections can never capture the full mystery of what it means to be human.

How I learned it

For years I believed feedback only flowed in one direction—downward. From the boss to the team. From the senior to the junior. From the evaluator to the evaluated. But life has a strange way of revealing that we are constantly shaping one another in ways we do not always see. And sometimes, the clearest mirror of who we are arrives years later, from someone we least expect.

Many years ago, I worked under a senior colleague based in the US—a man who, on every India visit, seemed determined to micromanage every detail of my work. Our interactions were battles, not loud, not emotional ones, but exhausting. I remember feeling that every small step forward required an argument, a justification, a fight for the integrity of the program. At that time, it felt like a tug-of-war of authority. I believed he simply did not trust me. What I did not realize was that something else entirely was happening beneath the surface.

Years later, when I was reshaping my online professional profile, I wrote to many former colleagues and supervisors requesting endorsements. Not one responded. Except him. His endorsement arrived unexpectedly—warm, generous, insightful. It was so surprising that I picked up the phone and asked the question that had lived quietly in me for years: "Why would you write this, when all we ever did was disagree?"

His answer was startling.

He said he never argued *against* me. He argued *through* me. He argued to learn. He argued to understand what risks he was blind to. He argued because he knew that if I held a position strongly, there was a reason worth examining. He argued because my pushback sharpened his judgement.

And then he said something I will never forget: "You were my rearview mirror. I learned India through your arguments. You helped me see what I could never have sensed sitting in another continent driving a program in India. That is why I endorsed you with all my heart."

We all have digital twins, but long before machines built them, humans were already doing it for each other.

Every debate, every disagreement, every reflection someone forces out of us becomes a piece of data—a behavioural trace that shapes us. My former boss became, unintentionally, a *human feedback loop*. He pushed me into clarity, into articulation, into deeper conviction. And I, without knowing it, became a learning system for him— filtering complexity, contextualizing India, sharpening his instincts.

Only years later, with distance and maturity, could I see it clearly: AI did not invent the feedback loop. It only scaled it. We have always evolved by mirroring, questioning, resisting and absorbing insights from those around us.

Today, our digital twins perform that role with dashboards, summaries, behavioural patterns and nudges. But my lesson is rooted in a time before algorithms: the quality of our evolution depends on the quality of the questions life asks us and the courage with which we answer them.

That is why owning our data matters. That is why conscious self-reflection matters. That is why intentionality matters. Because whether through a human mentor or an artificial one, we are always training something—our judgement, our clarity, our next version of ourselves. My former boss thought he was learning through me. I thought I was defending my work. In truth, we were strengthening each other's growth.

And that, ultimately, is what this chapter asks of every reader: to engage with your digital reflection—not passively, but courageously; to let your patterns teach you rather than trap you; to treat disagreement as data, and data as dialogue; and to remember that the journey towards a more conscious self begins with one simple act: looking at your reflection—human or digital—and choosing to learn from it.

10

CONNECTIONS ARE THE NEW CURRENCY

Your Network Will Determine Your Net Worth

Progress always has a price. Will you pay for it or will you profit from it?

What the coral reef teaches us about networking

"We cannot live only for ourselves. A thousand fibers connect us with our fellow men; and among those fibers, as sympathetic threads, our actions run as causes, and they come back to us as effects."

—Herman Melville

In the industrial age, land was the cornerstone of wealth. Owning land meant control, power and economic stability. The information age ushered in a shift, with data becoming the most coveted asset. But now, a new paradigm has emerged as we step into the network age, where connection itself is the most valuable resource because it fosters trust, collaboration and human relationships, which are essential for success in today's interconnected world. The true currency of our time isn't just how much information you have access to, but how effectively you can leverage your network to create value and make an impact. In today's world, connections are the new currency.

In the age of networks, connectivity goes far beyond the number of LinkedIn connections or X (formerly known as Twitter) followers we can boast about. It is no longer about who knows us, but rather about the depth and quality of the relationships we cultivate and maintain. It is about the flow of value, not just the static presence of contacts.

Who do you influence? Who influences you? Can you identify the right nodes in the network that can help you solve a problem, expand an idea or amplify an initiative? More importantly, how quickly can you convert an idea into action and impact by activating the right parts of your ecosystem?

Think about a coral reef. No single fish, coral, or structure can thrive in isolation. The reef flourishes because of the constant exchange of nutrients and signals, offering protection. Every organism in the reef plays a role in maintaining the balance of the ecosystem. The same principle applies to modern networks. A network, whether personal, professional or organizational, grows stronger and more resilient when there is continuous, dynamic interaction among its members.

The more diverse and engaged your connections are, the more anti-fragile your outcomes become. Because each connection brings a different perspective, resource or capability, your system gains the ability to adapt, recover and even improve when faced with shocks—rather than collapse under pressure. Like a coral reef, our network allows us to weather storms, quickly adapt to changes and bounce back stronger from setbacks. When things go wrong, the strength of our network can be the difference between collapse and recovery.

We are no longer solitary actors but interconnected nodes in a vast, planetary web. The tools of modern civilization, from communication platforms like Slack to collaborative open-source projects, have fundamentally altered how value is created and shared. We no longer live in silos, trying to build everything from scratch on our own. Instead, we are part of a collective intelligence that constantly flows and evolves.

Ideas are no longer confined to individual minds but are shared, refined and improved upon through collaborative efforts. This collective intelligence is not just about gathering data; it is about amplifying the impact of what is known through interaction and exchange.

This shift in how value is created means that individual knowledge is no longer the primary measure of success. In the past, knowledge acquisition and expertise were key indicators of one's professional standing. But in the network age, what truly matters is how well we can navigate systems, how effectively we can collaborate and how quickly we can translate information into action. The ability to connect the dots between different pieces of knowledge and to facilitate interactions that result in tangible outcomes is what defines success now.

In this interconnected world, our worth is no longer solely determined by what we know, but by how well we can leverage our connections to turn that knowledge into something actionable and impactful.

This new way of operating also has profound implications for how businesses, organizations and even individuals must think about growth and innovation. In today's economy, organizations that thrive are those that understand the importance of ecosystems, partnerships and collaborations. For example, the rise Amazon, Uber and Airbnb, shows how the network model can revolutionize entire industries. For example, Uber transformed the network model by turning every driver and rider into a node in a real-time, data-driven ecosystem—creating value not through owning assets, but by orchestrating continuous interaction between millions of independent participants.

These businesses do not own the resources they use; they connect people, services and assets in ways that create value across the system. By leveraging networks, these companies not only disrupted traditional business models but also redefined what it meant to be successful in the modern economy. For individuals, the importance of networks cannot be overstated. The network age demands a mindset shift: from one of individual achievement to one of collective success. It is not enough to just be good at your job or to have a single area of expertise. In this era, the ability to build, nurture and activate networks is one of the most valuable skills we can possess. Our network is a source of creativity, support and resilience, not just a tool for accessing opportunities.

We need to start asking ourselves a few key questions: Who are the ten closest people in my professional network? What problems are we solving together? How frequently does knowledge flow both ways between us? Am I merely consuming their expertise, or are am I actively contributing to the shared knowledge of the network? These questions are not just abstract metrics. They are the new return on investment we should be measuring in the networked world.

Building a robust, dynamic network is not a passive endeavour. It requires constant engagement, nurturing and a commitment to collaboration. Just as a coral reef thrives through symbiotic relationships, our professional network will flourish when it is built on mutual trust, reciprocity and shared goals. Success is about thriving together and leveraging the collective intelligence of our connections to create more value than we could ever produce on our own.

What ants teach us about collective intelligence

"Networking that matters is helping people achieve their goals."
—Seth Godin

The power of collective intelligence is not just theoretical. It is already here. Wikipedia is smarter than any individual contributor. Google search becomes more effective every second because every user improves the algorithm. Even Tesla cars improve together because they share driving data. Tesla's vehicles are not just machines; they are connected data centres that continuously gather data from sensors, cameras and other onboard devices. This data is then analyzed to optimize vehicle performance, improve safety and enhance intelligent features. The sharing of driving data among Tesla vehicles is a key aspect of their innovation strategy. Each vehicle acts as a data source, contributing to a global fleet that learns from diverse driving conditions and behaviours. This collective intelligence allows Tesla's AI systems to continuously improve, leading to better decision-making and safety in autonomous driving.

These are examples of scalable intelligence. Unlike our personal IQ, which is finite, collective intelligence is expandable; it grows with use; and it feeds itself.

Let us take a lesson from ants. One ant alone is feeble, forgetful and limited. But what about an ant colony? That is a super-organism. It builds bridges; finds food; moves mountains. Not because each ant is smart but because their communication is relentless.

Humans are similar. One person with a breakthrough idea could start a chain reaction. But the real magic emerges when that idea passes through the right network: early adopters, mentors, funders, critics and fans. That flow is what transforms ideas into revolutions.

In today's world, tools like GitHub, Notion and Figma are accelerators of collective intelligence. They allow designers, coders, writers and intellectuals to collaborate across geographies and time zones. The result? A constant upgrade loop.

Here is the twist: The more we contribute to collective intelligence, the more valuable we become. Not because of what we know, but because of how we enable knowledge to spread. Specifically, AI can be employed to enhance three elements of collective intelligence: collective memory, collective attention and collective reasoning. But collective intelligence has its pitfalls too—groups can amplify shared blind spots, spread errors faster or converge on the wrong conclusions if no one pauses to question the consensus.

So, the next time you are tempted to hoard an idea, ask yourself, *What happens if I share it?* If it thrives, so do you.

Your network is your net worth

In the industrial era, value came from our position; our title; our desk; our place in the assembly line. In the network era, value flows. It passes through connections, interactions and exchanges.

You may be brilliant, but if your ideas don't circulate, they stagnate. That is why open platforms outcompete closed ones. That is why a tweet can start a movement, a shared spreadsheet can map global supply chains and a WhatsApp group can launch a startup.

This shift requires a mindset change. Hoarding knowledge used to be power. Now, sharing it is. Because visibility is currency in networks. The more value we give away, the more people route opportunities our way. Generosity becomes a growth strategy.

Think of the most impactful educators, entrepreneurs or creators today. They don't just produce content; they produce context; they host conversations; they curate communities. They become hubs of insight—not just because of what they know, but because of what they enable.

Artificial intelligence accelerates this. Algorithms reward nodes that spark interaction. Platforms amplify those who generate value flow. In this world, you are not a resume; you are a relay.

Your net worth is a product of how you facilitate worth for others. How you amplify, connect and enrich the nodes around you.

In the end, the most valuable people are those who make others more valuable.

System literacy is the new literacy

It is no longer enough to be book smart. We need to be system smart.

- Systems literacy is not a subject. It is a stance.
- Sense the moment and act in rhythm with what is emerging.
- See beyond events and recognize the patterns shaping them.
- Feel the connections and honour the web of life that holds us all.
- Navigate tensions and hold space for paradox and polarity.
- Revere the ordinary and know that every action echoes in the whole.

System literacy is the ability to see interconnections where others see silos. It is understanding how a policy in one country affects agriculture in another; how a tweet influences stock prices; how a glitch in one node ripples through a global network.

We live in an age of cascading complexity. Climate change, pandemics, misinformation, economic volatility are not isolated problems; they are networked failures. And solving them requires networked minds.

That calls for the ability to map systems, not just memorize facts; to trace consequences; to understand paradoxes; to zoom in and out. System thinkers are more than just analysts; they are translators, designers and bridge-builders.

Bill Gates often says his learning is guided by understanding feedback loops. Harari reminds us that our fate will be decided not by individual choices, but by systemic shifts. How do we train our mind not just to store knowledge but to navigate systems?

Observe patterns. Ask: What causes this trend? What sustains it? Who benefits? Who is left out? System literacy is a muscle. The more we flex it, the less we react and the more we design.

In the nexus shift, our value lies in how well we interpret the invisible structures shaping the visible world.

Curate your network like your mind depends on it

We become who we surround ourselves with. That is not poetry. It is neuroscience.

Our network does not just influence what we learn. It shapes how we think. Our curiosity, our confidence, our creativity are deeply social. They rise or fall with your context.

The size of your network does not matter; it is the quality of your network that counts. The golden rule of networking is simple: don't keep score.

So it is not enough to network more. We have to network intentionally; choose who and what we plug into; follow people who challenge us; join groups that expand our horizon; and cut ties with echo chambers. At the same time, I want to share an insight here. Left unexamined, networks can just as easily narrow our thinking—rewarding conformity over curiosity, amplifying bias through repetition and quietly turning connection into a comfortable cage rather than a catalyst for growth.

Artificial intelligence offers endless personalization. But convenience is not clarity. Algorithms will loop our past unless we teach them to project our future. We must choose our inputs as deliberately as our outputs.

Curating our network means asking: Who uplifts me? Who sharpens me? Who calls out my blind spots? Who inspires action, not just thought? These are not merely social questions. They are survival questions in an age of distraction, disinformation and misinformation.

"Technology is a useful servant but a dangerous master."

—Christian Lous Lange

The good news is, networks are fluid. They grow as you grow. The more you contribute, the more you attract. The more you share, the more you learn. The more you listen, the more you evolve.

Our network is our ecosystem. Treat it like our future depends on it because it does.

How I learned it

I learned the true nature of networks—and how they shape behaviour—on a perfectly ordinary day that turned into a behavioural science case study. We were heading out as a family to visit a friend for lunch. I was feeling slightly low, the kids were taking forever to get ready, and in a moment of self-care I decided not to drive and booked a cab instead.

And then it happened.

Just as I was about to confirm the ride, a new "Tip Window" appeared—three neatly packaged options demanding a tip even before the service had begun. When I instinctively tried to skip it, the screen served me a line that instantly activated every behavioural antenna in my body: "I don't want to tip. I would like to wait."

It was no longer a suggestion. It was a nudge. A behavioural push wrapped in the language of choice.

Years of behavioural science chapters flashed before my eyes— each more alarming than the last. If I clicked "Tip," what would I really be doing?

- I would be revealing that time pressure makes me pliable.
- I would be signalling that urban Indian men above a certain age threshold are tip-compliant when stressed.
- I would be feeding the algorithm the ultimate behavioural goldmine: my vulnerability.
- And algorithms learn fast. One "yes" today, and tomorrow the "suggested tip" might quietly rise for all my Indian male comrades caught in weekend lunch-hour chaos.

The network was watching. And it never forgets.

The system wasn't just asking for money. It was asking for data about my threshold of surrender.

Just then, my wife—already exasperated by the delays— snapped, "Just pay it! We're getting late."

But I was no longer just a husband. I was a soldier of the data revolution. A freedom fighter in the Non-Cooperation Movement of 2025. A lone resistor standing against algorithmic tyranny.

I took a deep breath, steadied my trembling finger and clicked the boldest option of my adult life:

"I don't want to pay extra. I would like to wait."

Twenty full minutes appeared on the screen. Punishment, consequence or algorithmic retaliation—take your pick. My wife's eyes burned with the intensity of an exploding supernova. But I stood firm.

Because here is what I realized in that moment—an insight at the heart of this chapter:

- *Every node affects the system.* My refusal influenced the pricing dynamics of thousands like me.

- *Every decision contributes to collective intelligence.* Algorithms learn not just from what we choose, but from what we reject.

- *Connections create consequences.* My choice rippled across a vast consumer network, a reminder that our behaviour is never isolated.

- *Power lies not in what we know, but in how we participate.* My refusal was not about ₹30. It was about agency—about who shapes whom in a connected world.

- *Networks amplify everything—wisdom, fear and pressure.* My wife's glare alone could have rebooted the system.

And most importantly: you are never acting alone. In a networked world, every action is a signal, every signal becomes data and every data point shapes the future.

Ethics and intention now matter more than ever. If we look through the event, we will find that woven through all of this was one quiet realization: ethics and intention now matter more than ever. In a networked world, even small choices shape larger patterns. A single tap can normalize a manipulative design or challenge it. Every refusal, every acceptance, every hesitation becomes a signal the system learns from. When our behaviour trains the machine, doing the "right thing" is no longer a private virtue it becomes a public responsibility. In the age of AI, intention is influence.

That day taught me that networks don't just connect us they interpret us. They infer, adapt and evolve based on how we move, hesitate, resist or comply. The intelligence of the network depends on what we feed it. And sometimes, the most powerful contribution we can make to collective intelligence is a simple, stubborn act of refusal.

So yes, our cab arrived 20 minutes late. Yes, my wife considered feeding *me* to the algorithm. But I walked away with the most important lesson of this chapter: your net worth is not just who you know—it is also what you signal to the networks that know you. And sometimes, resistance is the most valuable signal of all.

THE INVISIBLE FAULT LINE

Surviving the AI Divide and Displacement Dilemma

The future will not be decided by what machines can do, but by what humans refuse to surrender.

Job loss is gradual but profound

Recently, Nvidia CEO Jensen Huang said that artificial intelligence will not lead to mass layoffs, but it will transform the nature of various jobs. On the other hand, Bill Gates feels that humans may soon not be needed "for most things", while Elon Musk believes most people won't have to work at all in twenty years. But Geoffrey Hinton feels that all these predictions are overlooking one major reality that AI may cause economic upheaval which may lead to mass unemployment. As reported by *Fortune*, speaking at the Georgetown University along with Bernie Sanders, Hinton said that the tech giants are busy investing trillions in data centres and chips and are heavily betting on AI systems which can replace human labour at lower cost. Hinton has become increasingly vocal about what he sees as Big Tech's misplaced priorities, arguing that the industry is driven more by short-term profits than scientific progress.

The financial realities of AI are also becoming a cause of concern. ChatGPT creator OpenAI is not expected to turn a profit until at least 2030 and may need more than $207 billion to sustain growth, according to HSBC estimates.

Hinton who left Google in 2023 in order to speak freely about the risks of AI. He warned that AI will lead to new job creation but it will not offset the scale of losses

The impacts of AI are beginning to reshape industries, economies and job markets at an accelerating pace. The disruption starts with the automation of repetitive tasks but does not stop there. As machine learning becomes cheaper, more capable and more widespread, we are seeing entire job categories disappear. The result is a phenomenon that Hinton calls "the invisible fault line", a disruption that does not announce itself with fanfare but instead manifests slowly, almost imperceptibly. For example, truck drivers, once the backbone of logistics, are being replaced by autonomous vehicles. Similarly, workers in call centres are being displaced by conversational agents that can handle customer queries more efficiently and accurately. Many companies, including banks and airlines, have adopted AI chatbots to manage customer inquiries and resolve common issues 24/7, reducing the need for human customer service representatives. AI-powered robots in warehouses, such as those used by Amazon, automate tasks like sorting and packaging, leading to fewer manual labour jobs in logistics. Even jobs in creative fields, such as copywriting, are at risk as AI-driven generative models can churn out text that imitates human writing.

The human cost of this disruption is stark, and it does not just affect those directly displaced. Communities that rely on jobs with routine tasks for income are at risk of becoming economically marginalized. Moreover, this is not a sudden, catastrophic collapse but a gradual erosion of livelihoods. The true cruelty lies in the fact that workers don't lose their jobs overnight; they are slowly rendered unnecessary. As we edge further into an AI-driven world, more and more people will experience this slow displacement. The most vulnerable—those who lack the resources to re-skill or adapt—will be left behind, creating deeper divides in society.

The implications of this fault line extend beyond the workforce. Artificial intelligence's disruption does not just affect the job market; it has the potential to destabilize economies and alter the social fabric of entire nations. The first wave of AI integration into the economy might appear as a win for productivity, but as more sectors are affected, it will become clear that these changes bring significant costs. For industries, businesses and governments, ignoring this shift is not an option. As Hinton warns, the threat is not a distant spectre but a present reality. Sanders also raised concerns about AI's impact on human relationships, noting that teenagers increasingly rely on AI companions. "If kids today have AI as their best friends … what kind of change does that mean for humanity?"

While Gates and Musk envision a future where humans are freed from work, Hinton insists the conversation must also address the social and economic consequences of mass displacement.

To avoid the potential fallout of this shift, we need to confront the truth head-on. The foundation of work, economic stability and even social trust is being challenged by AI. It is imperative that we understand the fault lines, as failing to recognize them means risking falling into them without even knowing it.

Reset inequality by design

Yuval Harari has long warned about the dangers of technology amplifying human flaws. Algorithms, while often regarded as impartial and objective tools, are reflections of the biases and power structures that exist in the world. Artificial intelligence is not an exception to this rule—if anything, it may be the most potent example. What we often fail to recognize is that AI systems are only as good as the data they are trained on. Unfortunately, much of this data is tainted with the prejudices and inequalities that permeate society.

Artificial intelligence systems don't have an inherent sense of fairness or justice. They do not possess moral compasses or ethical guidelines. Instead, they rely on vast amounts of data upon which they learn to make decisions. But if the data reflects systemic biases—whether based on race, gender, socioeconomic status or geographic location—the AI will inherently reinforce those biases. For instance, predictive policing algorithms that disproportionately target minority communities are not doing so because the system has "decided" to be unfair. Instead, they are reflecting historical patterns of policing, which have been biased. These are not flaws in the algorithms themselves, but rather flaws in the underlying systems they are designed to replicate.

One of the most insidious aspects of algorithmic bias is that it is often invisible. The decisions made by algorithms are presented as objective and data-driven, which makes them feel legitimate and indisputable. People trust algorithms because they seem to be grounded in logic and mathematics—disciplines that are often seen as impartial. But when the data driving these systems is flawed, the outcomes they produce are also flawed, only at a much larger scale and much faster rate. This illusion of objectivity makes it difficult to challenge or question algorithmic decisions, further entrenching inequality.

Artificial intelligence's capacity to encode and amplify inequality extends beyond individual instances of biased decision-making. At a societal level, the very design of AI systems can exacerbate social divides. Those who have access to high-quality education, data literacy and digital infrastructure are the ones who benefit from AI. Conversely, those without these privileges are at risk of being left behind. As AI becomes increasingly integrated into every aspect of life—from healthcare and education to hiring and law enforcement—the gap between the haves and have-nots is likely to widen, creating a more stratified society.

To avoid this outcome, we must demand greater transparency in AI systems. Developers must be held accountable for ensuring that the data they use is diverse, representative and free from bias. Algorithms must be audited regularly to ensure they are not inadvertently perpetuating inequality. Moreover, it is crucial that we teach digital literacy and critical thinking from an early age. The next generation must be equipped to recognize and challenge algorithmic biases in the systems that will increasingly shape their lives.

Human capital in an age of machines

The rapid advancement of AI has sparked fears of obsolescence. As machines become increasingly capable of performing tasks traditionally reserved for humans—ranging from data analysis to creative expression—there is an underlying anxiety about what role humans will play in the workforce of the future. Will there be any place for human expertise when AI can outperform us in so many domains?

However, the answer is not to compete with machines but to complement them. The future of work lies not in resisting technological change, but in harnessing our uniquely human traits to work alongside AI. Machines may excel at processing vast amounts of data, recognizing patterns and even generating content, but they still lack the creativity, emotional intelligence and ethical judgement that are essential to the human experience. These qualities are not just "soft skills" but critical to success in an AI-driven world.

Microsoft CEO Satya Nadella has underscored that emotional intelligence is becoming increasingly vital as AI assumes more technical responsibilities. Nadella reiterated his belief that empathy is a critical business skill and not merely a peripheral soft skill. Nadella highlighted that leaders who lack emotional intelligence risk underutilising their potential in an AI-driven environment. Under Nadella's leadership, Microsoft has embraced a "growth mindset", shifting from a "know-it-all" to a "learn-it-all" culture. This transformation has been pivotal in Microsoft's success, with its stock rising nearly 20 per cent this year and its valuation reaching $3.7 trillion. The company's focus on blending emotional intelligence with AI-driven collaboration reflects its evolving workplace philosophy.

In particular, emotional intelligence is becoming increasingly important. It encompasses self-awareness, empathy and the ability to navigate complex social interactions. These skills are critical in leadership, collaboration and customer service, areas where machines cannot replicate human touch. Artificial intelligence cannot understand the nuances of human relationships or offer the empathy that is often needed in high-stakes environments, such as healthcare, education and conflict resolution.

In addition to emotional intelligence, another key human skill is interdisciplinary curiosity—the ability to integrate knowledge from different fields and apply it creatively. As AI automates routine tasks, the professionals who will thrive in the future are those who can adapt quickly, think critically and move across domains with ease. Lifelong learning is no longer a luxury but a necessity. The job market of the future will demand people who are not only highly skilled, but also continuously evolving.

Governments, employers and individuals all have a role to play in fostering human capital. Governments must invest in education systems that emphasize creativity, critical thinking and adaptability. Employers must view upskilling as an investment, not an expense, and offer opportunities for employees to learn new skills. Finally, individuals must take ownership of their learning journey, seeking out opportunities for growth and being proactive about their skill development.

As we enter the AI age, the most successful people will be those who can integrate human insight with machine intelligence. Rather than fearing obsolescence, we must embrace our unique abilities and find ways to work in tandem with technology to unlock new possibilities.

How to remain indispensable in your job

According to the World Economic Forum, it is estimated that, by 2030, 39 per cent of workers' existing skill sets will be outdated, and about 59 per cent of today's workforce will need training to stay current. Artificial intelligence is quickly taking on tasks that we are used to doing ourselves. And this means that our roles will shift. Writers will become editors. Doers will become reviewers. Job titles will mean less while our ability to flex, be creative, build new skills, and leverage new technology will mean more.

What is unfolding is not the disappearance of work, but the redefinition of value within it. As machines absorb execution-heavy tasks, the human contribution shifts upward—from producing outputs to shaping intent. Professionals will be expected to frame better questions, evaluate machine-generated options and apply judgement where context matters. The premium will move from speed to sense-making, from compliance to creativity. Roles will blur, hierarchies will flatten and adaptability will outweigh specialization. In this new order, relevance will belong not to those who cling to titles, but to those who continuously reconfigure their skills alongside evolving technologies.

In the evolving order of the intelligent machine age, indispensability no longer belongs to the strongest executors of tasks, but to those who embody and express the deepest layers of the human condition. The illusion of irreplaceability by output is dissolving rapidly. Machines now code, paint, analyze and even respond with convincing empathy in customer service chats. But they do not form trust. They do not carry the weight of lived contradiction. They do not sit in silence and hear what was not said.

Being indispensable in the AI era requires moving beyond function to embrace human value at its most textured. This is not a sentimental retreat to nostalgia; it is a strategic positioning in a system whose every advance exposes the void machines cannot fill.

True indispensability is built at the crossroads of qualities that resist automation: creativity that is informed by cultural nuance, empathy that adapts in real-time to shifting human emotion, collaboration that builds on the invisible energy between people and storytelling that reveals not just what happened, but what it meant.

These are not soft skills; they are survival skills in a world increasingly shaped by cold logic.

The rise of AI is not eliminating jobs; it is redefining roles. The future will not be owned by deep specialists alone, but by agile generalists who think across silos, merge perspectives and challenge boundaries. A systems designer who also understands anthropology. A machine learning engineer who grasps the poetry of language. A data analyst who senses political undercurrents. These are the hybrids who will shape the horizon.

Moreover, indispensability will emerge from clarity of purpose. People who can articulate the "why" behind a system, who inspire loyalty not through authority but through shared intention, who hold communities together not by command but by narrative— these humans will become not just necessary, but central to any socio-technical ecosystem.

In a reality mediated by machines, human presence is elevated to something more than a tool; it becomes a compass. Trust will be the new currency. Ambiguity will be the new terrain. And those who can walk into uncertainty not with fear, but with a framework for meaning, will guide others forward.

Thus, to become indispensable is not to compete against AI on its terms. It is to rise into uniquely human dimensions—connection, purpose, synthesis—that no line of code can emulate.

In this sense, the most vital professionals of the coming age will be those who are not just skilled, but deeply aware of themselves, of others and of the narratives that bind us all to a future we must collectively create.

Having said that, basic AI literacy is required. It is the new Excel for professionals.

Systemic safeguards for a shared future

As AI grows in scope and consequence, the question is no longer whether societies will be transformed but how equitably, how ethically and for whom. The future does not only demand smarter machines; it demands wiser systems.

To secure a human-centred tomorrow, systemic safeguards must become more than aspirational—they must become foundational. The aim is not to resist progress, but to channel it through justice.

Public policy will be the first frontier. Governments must move from reactive regulation to proactive redesign. Universal basic income, once viewed as radical, is increasingly seen as a pragmatic buffer for a workforce in transition. But this is not just economic cushioning; it is moral architecture. A guaranteed income for all could address AI and automation's most pressing challenges: wage inequality, job insecurity and widespread job losses. The automation revolution demands a new social contract where technological progress and human welfare advance together rather than at each other's expense. It reflects an acknowledgment that labour will no longer be the only metric of dignity.

Artificial intelligence impact audits must become routine. Just as companies are held accountable for environmental damage, they must now be accountable for algorithmic harm. Transparency in data sourcing, clarity in model bias, explainability in decisions cannot be optional. They are ethical imperatives in an age where unseen code increasingly governs seen realities.

Corporations must evolve too. No longer can ethical reflection be confined to corporate social responsibility departments or quarterly compliance checklists. Ethics must become a design input, embedded into product teams, marketing decisions, hiring algorithms and leadership frameworks. The organizations that thrive will be those that treat responsibility not as friction, but as innovation's partner.

Education must likewise be re-engineered. It is not enough to teach students how to use AI. They must be equipped to interrogate it, question its defaults and redesign it for better human outcomes. Curricula must shift from content mastery to context awareness; from knowing facts to understanding frameworks. A generation raised by search engines must be taught how to search meaningfully.

And beyond all this, lies the planetary imperative.

The global AI landscape is fragmented, with a few nations leading, some striving to catch up and many excluded, amplifying economic and social disparities. In the Global South, limited access to energy-intensive AI infrastructure, advanced computing capabilities, high-quality data and AI skills hinder nations from reaping the economic and societal benefits that AI can offer. The growing global AI gap is projected to perpetuate economic disparities and social inequalities and affect international competitiveness.

The pursuit of AI maturity is not merely a technological endeavour; it is becoming a strategic imperative for driving innovation and growth across all economic sectors, promoting societal advancement and increasing global competitiveness.

Artificial intelligence is not contained by borders. Its implications ripple globally, often amplifying inequalities between regions with tech sovereignty and those without. Global cooperation is not a diplomatic luxury; it is survival strategy. Shared research standards, international treaties on AI safety, collaborative ethics boards are not fantasies. They are necessities if the species wishes to remain in charge of its own evolution.

To design systemic safeguards is to acknowledge that no machine, no matter how powerful, will act ethically by default. Only human structures, designed with foresight and courage, can create the frameworks where intelligence serves humanity, not the other way around. Global cooperation is essential to ensure that AI develops as a shared good, not a divisive force.

The AI value chain is inherently global and the challenges faced in achieving AI maturity are frequently shared across geographical regions. All nations are looking to increase their global competitiveness through AI adoption and innovation. But the road to success is paved with complexity and requires agile decision-making and holistic strategies.

In 2024, the AI Governance Alliance, part of the World Economic Forum's Centre for the Fourth Industrial Revolution, introduced the AI Competitiveness through Regional Collaboration initiative. It aims to guide regions and nations in the complex process of designing and implementing holistic strategies to harness the benefits of AI, build competitiveness and realize prosperity for all.

This century's greatest challenge is not technological; it is civilizational. And the systems built today will determine whether AI becomes our servant, our partner or our sovereign.

How I learned it

There are moments in history when technology does not arrive with drama or thunder, but with paperwork. It enters quietly through new machines in a back room, new job titles on office doors, new skills whispered about in corridors. And by the time people realize what has changed, the old world is already gone. I learned this lesson not from a futuristic lab or a Silicon Valley boardroom, but from the life of a woman who lived decades before the word AI entered our vocabulary: Katherine Coleman Goble Johnson.

Johnson was a mathematician at NASA at a time when neither women nor black professionals were expected to shape the future of space travel. In the 1950s and early 60s, her job title was "computer"—not a machine, but a human being who performed calculations by hand. Then, quietly, machines arrived. IBM mainframes entered NASA's corridors, threatening to replace entire rooms of human calculators. For many, this was the beginning of fear and obsolescence. For Katherine, it was a signal.

What moved me deeply when I first encountered her story— later immortalized in the film *Hidden Figures*—was not just her brilliance, but her response to change. She did not resist the machines. She did not romanticize the old ways. Instead, she did something far more courageous: she *learned*. She taught herself programming. She insisted on understanding how the computers worked, what assumptions they made and where they could fail. And when astronauts like John Glenn refused to trust machine outputs without human verification, it was Johnson they asked to check the numbers. Not because she was faster than the computer but because she brought judgement, context and responsibility into the equation.

That, for me, is the precise emotional and intellectual heart of this chapter.

Johnson understood something many of us still struggle with today: displacement is rarely sudden; it is gradual and silent. The threat was not that computers would immediately take her job. The threat was that those who did not learn to work *with* them would slowly become irrelevant. Her genius lay not only in mathematics, but also in timing. She upgraded herself before the wave hit. And in doing so, she transformed from a replaceable role into an irreplaceable mind. But she did not stop there. She quietly urged other black women in her unit to stay back after hours, to learn programming and understand the machines so that the future would not arrive for her alone, but for all of them together.

I learned from her life that skills are perishable. What saves us is not what we know, but how quickly and willingly we evolve when the ground shifts beneath us. Johnson did not wait for permission to learn. She did not ask whether learning programming was in her job description. She understood that dignity in a changing system comes from agency, not entitlement.

This lesson mirrors the central argument of this chapter: AI disruption is not theoretical; it is already rearranging power, opportunity and identity. Automation often looks harmless at first— an efficiency tool, a support system, a backend upgrade. But like those early NASA computers, once embedded, it quietly redraws who matters and who doesn't. Those who treat new technologies as someone else's problem eventually discover it has become *their* problem.

What also struck me deeply about Johnson's story is that she did not succeed alone. She brought others with her. She encouraged fellow black women mathematicians to learn programming, to step into the machine rooms, to claim space where exclusion had been normalized. This was not just reskilling; it was collective resilience. It was an early model of inclusive adaptation—something we urgently need as AI threatens to widen existing inequalities.

Her story also reminds us why the final frontiers of human value—empathy, story, judgement and context—matter more now, not less. Computers could calculate trajectories faster, but they could not understand what failure meant when human lives were on the line. They could process inputs, but they could not carry moral weight. Johnson's numbers mattered because *she* mattered— her calculations were infused with accountability, lived experience and care.

When I reflect on my own professional life, this story has become a quiet compass. Every time a new technology emerges, every time a tool promises to "optimize" or "replace", I ask myself the same question Johnson answered decades ago: *Am I resisting the change, or am I learning fast enough to stay ahead of it?* The future does not punish those who are less gifted. It punishes those who are slower to adapt.

This chapter is ultimately not about fear of superintelligence. It is about preparedness of human intelligence. Johnson did not survive the technological shift because she was extraordinary—though she was—but because she acted in time. She recognized the wave early, paddled hard and learned to ride it rather than be crushed by it.

That is the lesson I carry forward: timely learning is the most humane form of self-preservation. The question is not whether machines will change our work; they already have. The real question is whether we will do what Katherine Johnson did—step forward, learn bravely and claim our place in a future that is being written with or without us.

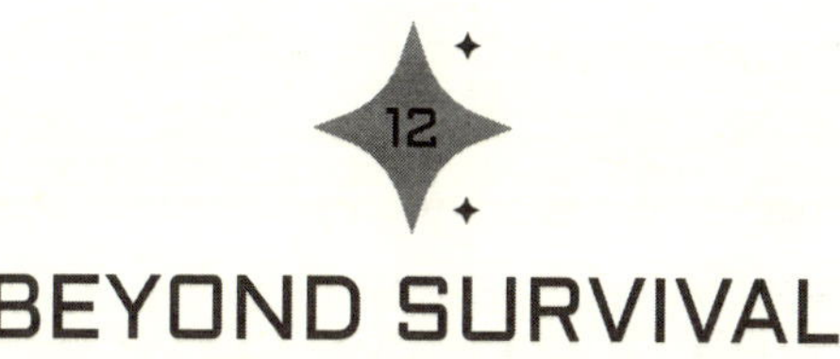

BEYOND SURVIVAL

Becoming the Human AI Cannot Replace

It is not about resisting the wave. It is about becoming the surfer others follow.

Why human uniqueness still matters

"We need to build AI that makes humanity better, not replace it."
—Sam Altman

What makes us irreplaceably human? Artificial intelligence writes stories, paints pictures, predicts diseases and even imitates friendship. And yet, beneath the veneer of intelligence, there is a crucial difference—a soul-level gap. This gap is not just philosophical; it is strategic. Understanding it might be the key to surviving and thriving in the age of artificial intelligence.

What truly separates humans from machines isn't raw processing power; it is the messiness of emotion, the nuance of ethics, the complexity of culture. Machines can be trained to imitate empathy, but imitation is not meaning. A chatbot can say, "I'm sorry for your loss," but it doesn't feel the silence that follows. It doesn't feel the lump in your throat, the chill of absence or the gentle ache of memory.

True empathy arises not from scripts, but from shared suffering and compassion. In hospitals, schools, families and communities humans still hold the upper hand. Empathy fuels trust. Trust fuels relationships. And relationships are the bedrock of society.

Equally irreplaceable is the domain of ethical judgement. While AI can process the letter of the law, it does not understand the spirit behind it. Algorithms do not have morals; they have instructions. An AI may optimize for outcomes, but it cannot reflect on what *ought* to be done. Morality, justice and social accountability emerge from lived realities, historical pain and cultural memory where human consciousness still reigns.

Creativity, too, holds its own as a frontier. Yes, AI can compose music or design logos, but it lacks context. It lacks suffering, longing, humour, rebellion and love—the drivers behind great art and innovation. Human creativity is not just about generating outputs; it is about expressing identity just like a protest mural that carries the scars of a neighbourhood, or a folk song that preserves a community's memory long after its people have moved on. Art is often an act of healing, protest or spiritual seeking. Can a machine ever know what it means to sing because your grandmother did? To paint because your country was at war? To write because your heart was broken?

In the coming decade, machines will become better at doing tasks, but being human will become more important than ever. Our ability to sit with uncertainty, wrestle with paradox and make decisions rooted in conscience is not a limitation; it is our final edge.

So, rather than competing with machines on their turf, we must double down on ours. We must protect and practise the skills that no machine can replicate—empathy, ethics and existential creativity. In doing so, we not only preserve our relevance, we define our role in a future that is increasingly shared with machines.

This is the final frontier. Not the race for faster algorithms, but the rediscovery of slower, deeper truths. Not automation, but augmentation. Not substitution, but symbiosis. What makes us human isn't what we do; it is why and how we do it.

Strategic thinking in the age of AI

"One of the most important things I have learned is that businesses don't need new technology; they need a new mindset."

—Satya Nadella

Strategic thinking has always been a differentiator. But in a world increasingly shaped by AI, it is rapidly becoming non-negotiable. Artificial intelligence can tell you what is happening, even what might happen next. But it cannot tell you what matters, what aligns with your values, or what is worth fighting for. That job still belongs to the human strategist.

Strategic thinking is not just long-term planning; it is moral navigation. It involves seeing through complexity, anticipating consequences and aligning today's choices with tomorrow's vision. This is where humans shine. Artificial intelligence can analyze options, but humans must define meaning.

Consider a CEO deciding whether to automate a factory. The data might show massive short-term profit, but what about the long-term impact on community morale? On worker dignity? On consumer perception? These are ethical questions, not spreadsheet ones. And they demand human judgement.

Strategic thinking also means adaptability. In the past, strategies were set like blueprints. Today, they must be drawn like maps in sand—flexible, provisional, responsive. We need to think in loops, not lines. Test, learn, adapt. This is not a weakness; it is an evolutionary advantage.

In this new world, every professional from teacher to trader, marketer to policymaker must become a systems thinker. It is no longer enough to be an expert in our silos. We must understand how our decisions ripple outward through culture, society and technology.

Importantly, strategic thinkers must learn to speak both languages—the human and the machine. They must know how to interpret model outputs, but also when to challenge them. They must understand that data is not destiny and that correlation is not causation.

This is the essence of Karpathy's idea behind Software 2.0: software that writes itself, adapts, evolves. In this world, the best professionals will not merely consume AI; they will co-steer it. They will shape the questions that shape the answers.

So how do you build strategic muscle? You ask better questions. You map possibilities. You look at trade-offs. You step back from tasks and ask about systems. You become less reactive and more reflective.

This skill is not learned overnight. It is cultivated. It is about habit, humility and horizon-scanning. It is about thinking not just about what works but what matters.

Emotional intelligence—the human edge

While machines can process emotions, only humans can truly feel them. This distinction though subtle but profound is what makes EI our enduring superpower in the age of AI. In workplaces increasingly saturated with automation and analytics, it is EI that anchors trust, collaboration and resilience.

Emotional intelligence is not just about being "nice", it is about being deeply self-aware. It is about understanding our triggers, managing our reactions and empathizing with others even when it is inconvenient. These are the soft skills that hold hard decisions together. Consider a startup founder facing a sudden revenue shortfall. The data suggests immediate layoffs. A founder with low EI reacts defensively or impulsively, cutting teams without communication and eroding trust overnight. A founder with high EI pauses, acknowledges the fear, listens to the team, communicates transparently, explores shared sacrifice and carries people through uncertainty with dignity. The decision may still be painful, but the way it is handled preserves morale, loyalty and long-term resilience. That difference is EI at work.

Let us start with self-awareness. Artificial intelligence can detect stress in our voice, but only we can decide what that means. Only we can connect it to childhood insecurities, current fears or unspoken hopes. Self-awareness is the beginning of mastery. It is also the antidote to manipulation in a world where algorithms know our patterns better than we do.

Then comes empathy. Leaders who embody empathy inspire loyalty. Teachers who practise it transform students. Parents who model it raise resilient kids. In an age of remote work, digital classrooms and virtual therapy, empathy is no longer optional; it is structural.

Emotional intelligence also drives conflict resolution. Artificial intelligence can detect tension in emails or analyze sentiment on social media. But resolving conflict—navigating hurt, misunderstanding and pride—still requires the human heart; the courage to apologize; the wisdom to forgive; the foresight to prevent.

Emotional intelligence is the differentiator in hiring, promoting, selling and serving. A machine might sort resumes, but only a human can spot potential behind a poor interview. Artificial intelligence might script a sales pitch, but only a human can pivot in the moment when a client's eyes glaze over.

What is exciting is that EI can be taught and trained. Through feedback, reflection, coaching and mindfulness, we can strengthen our ability to understand ourselves and others.

In a world chasing speed, EI invites us to slow down; to listen more deeply; to connect more authentically; and to remember that beyond algorithms and automation, every system we build is meant to serve people.

So while machines may rise, it is EI that will rise with us. Artificial intelligence will never replace love unless it can figure out how to text back on time.

Adapting in a dynamic world

"The illiterate of the twenty-first century will not be those who cannot read and write but those who cannot learn, unlearn and relearn."

—Alvin Toffler

In an earlier time, learning had a finish line. We graduated, got a job and relied on that accumulated knowledge for decades. But in today's fast-changing world, learning is a lifestyle.

Artificial intelligence is advancing faster than any educational curriculum can keep pace. Skills we once thought were essential are becoming outdated within years—sometimes even months. Take coding, for example. A decade ago, it was a prized skill. Today, no-code platforms and AI-assisted development tools are reducing the barrier to entry. Tomorrow, even that might seem quaint. This does not mean that skills are irrelevant; it means they are not enough. The deeper skill is how to learn, unlearn and relearn.

Lifelong learning begins with a mindset. It is about curiosity, humility and resilience. It means being open to feedback, questioning one's assumptions and embracing discomfort. More importantly, it is about intentionally designing learning environments around us by joining cohorts, using AI tools like personalized tutors, curating our own curriculum from podcasts, papers and people.

Unlearning is equally critical. The habits and knowledge that helped us succeed yesterday may be the very ones holding us back today. Lifelong learners ask themselves regularly: "What do I need to let go of?"

In the AI age, where machines can quickly absorb and replicate human knowledge, the human edge lies in meta-learning—knowing how to learn faster, more effectively and more creatively than ever before. This shift is not a luxury; it is survival.

Ethical leadership in the digital age

"Scale your reach without scaling out your humanity."
—Neil Patel

As AI becomes embedded in everyday life, leadership must evolve with it. We have entered a new moral frontier where decisions made in boardrooms and codebases affect lives in real-time at scale and often invisibly. And in this frontier, ethical leadership is not optional; it is essential.

Artificial intelligence does not possess a moral compass. It does not weigh empathy against efficiency. It does not know when to bend a rule to save a life. These judgements remain human territory. But algorithms are being deployed in areas like policing, hiring, lending and medicine that are steeped in moral complexity. Without careful human oversight, AI can perpetuate bias, strip privacy or widen inequality.

This puts an urgent responsibility on today's leaders to innovate, and to guide that innovation with integrity. Ethical leadership means asking hard questions: Is this technology fair? Is it inclusive? Does it empower or exploit? It also means resisting the allure of short-term gains when they conflict with long-term human values.

Leaders must also invest in AI literacy for themselves and their teams. We can't govern what we don't understand. Knowing how algorithms work (and fail) is as important as knowing how markets move or people think.

Perhaps most critically, ethical leadership in the digital age is about transparency. The more open an organization is about how it uses AI to collect data, how it is analyzed and how decisions are made—the more trust it builds.

In short, tomorrow's most successful leaders will not be those who race ahead with technology. They will be those who lead it responsibly, ethically and with human dignity at the centre.

Humans and machines—collaborating together

The debate about AI often paints a binary picture: Will machines replace humans, or won't they? But the truth is far more nuanced and far more hopeful. The future doesn't belong to AI or to humans. It belongs to collaborative intelligence where both amplify each other's strengths.

Machines are unparalleled at crunching data, detecting patterns and optimizing decisions at scale. Humans, on the other hand, bring intuition, ethics, empathy and imagination to the table. The most exciting developments are happening at the intersection of these strengths.

In healthcare, AI can scan millions of radiology images in minutes, spotting anomalies with remarkable precision. But it is still the doctor who reads the context—the patient's history, fears, environment—and makes the final call. In journalism, AI can draft articles or analyze sentiment, but human editors decide which narratives matter, what tone to take and which questions to ask.

This partnership is not just tactical; it is philosophical. It challenges us to redefine work as a set of capabilities, not a list of tasks. Which parts of your job are uniquely human? Which can be shared with a machine? Which can be reimagined entirely? Consider the role of an urban planner. Traditionally, the job involved zoning regulations, traffic projections and long approval cycles. Today, AI can simulate population growth, model traffic flows, predict environmental impact and generate multiple design scenarios in seconds. But the planner's true value no longer lies in crunching these variables. It lies in judgement: deciding whose mobility matters most, how public spaces foster dignity and belonging, and which trade-offs a city is willing to live with for decades. The machine can propose efficient cities; only humans can envision humane ones. Here, work is no longer about executing plans, but about *choosing futures*—a responsibility that cannot be automated.

Collaboration with AI also demands new soft skills: prompt engineering, critical questioning and ethical evaluation. Teams that include both humans and machines must learn to communicate across that boundary. It is not just about feeding data in; it is about interpreting what comes out.

Ultimately, collaborative intelligence shifts our perspective from control to coordination, from mastery to partnership. It allows us to stop fearing obsolescence and start designing relevance.

Creativity and innovation beyond algorithms

"The creative part, the surprising part, the breaking-the-rules part—that is not AI. That's us."

—Seth Godin

Algorithms are good at remixing what already exists. They can draw from vast databases of art, music and language to generate novel combinations. But true innovation does not just remix the past—it disrupts it. And that is still a deeply human endeavour.

Creativity is not just output; it is about input—lived experience, emotional nuance, cultural insight and deep curiosity. Machines don't daydream; they don't reflect on childhood, experience awe or wrestle with meaning. These are the raw materials of human imagination.

Innovation is also about risk-taking. Artificial intelligence plays it statistically safe. It avoids outliers. Humans, on the other hand, stumble into breakthroughs because we are irrational, emotional and have intuition. Every major innovation—electricity, flight, the internet—came from dreams, not just data.

"On the morning the truth began to unstitch itself, Leonard felt a faint, traitorous thrill, as if the world had agreed to tilt a fraction in his favour."

If you are thinking, well that sounds a lot like the opening sentence of a new Ian McEwan novel, you would be half-right. Rather it is a sentence written *in the style* of Ian McEwan, as generated by a free-to-use AI platform. Admittedly, the prose is a little too florid for an author who wields his pen more like a scalpel. And yet on the surface and to your average reader, it is a passable approximation of his work.

You can understand why, according to a new study by Cambridge University, more than half of published novelists in the UK agree that it is likely AI will displace their work entirely. This isn't anything new: for months if not years, novelists have expressed their growing unease about the speed and scale of AI's trespass into the literary world.

Yuval Harari in an interview to Ritula Shah in London in September 2025 said that his next book will be the last as AI will soon take over authoring books.

The good news? Artificial intelligence can supercharge human creativity. It can draft prototypes, offer unexpected connections or simulate future scenarios. It is a tool for the creative process, not a substitute for it. At the end of the day, as much as an AI-generated sentence might look and sound like an Ian McEwan sentence, it will never be one. At the end of the day, people will always want those human voices. The best creators of tomorrow will treat AI not as a threat, but as a collaborator—a kind of muse with a very large database.

Organizations, too, must design for innovation. That means encouraging psychological safety (so people take risks), diverse perspectives (so blind spots shrink) and iterative exploration (so failure becomes part of progress).

In short, creativity in the AI era is not about keeping up with machines; it is about going where machines can't yet. That unexplored frontier is still very much human.

Building resilience in the face of change

"We're going to see more change in the next five years than we've seen in the last fifty."

—Jack Ma

Change is the only constant in our rapidly evolving world. The rise of AI has accelerated this transformation, reshaping industries, redefining job roles and challenging our traditional ways of thinking.

In such a dynamic environment, resilience becomes not just a desirable trait but a necessary skill.

Resilience is the capacity to recover quickly from difficulties and adapt to new circumstances. It is about maintaining equilibrium in the face of adversity and emerging stronger from challenges. Building resilience involves cultivating a growth mindset, where setbacks are viewed as opportunities for learning and development. This perspective encourages individuals to embrace change rather than fear it.

Developing resilience also requires emotional intelligence. Understanding and managing one's emotions, as well as empathizing with others, fosters a supportive environment where individuals can navigate change collaboratively. Effective communication, active listening and empathy are crucial components of this process.

Moreover, resilience is bolstered by a strong support network. Engaging with mentors, peers and professional communities provides a safety net during times of uncertainty. These connections offer guidance, encouragement and diverse perspectives that can illuminate new paths forward.

In the context of AI, resilience entails staying informed about technological advancements and being willing to upskill or reskill as needed. It means recognizing the potential of AI to augment human capabilities rather than replace them. By adopting a proactive approach to learning and development, individuals can position themselves to thrive alongside AI.

Ultimately, building resilience is about embracing change as an integral part of growth. It is about developing the mental and emotional fortitude to face challenges head-on, adapting to new realities, and continuing to move forward with purpose and determination.

Ethical decision-making

"The development of AI is as fundamental as the creation of the microprocessor, the personal computer, the Internet and the mobile phone."

—Bill Gates

As AI systems become increasingly integrated into our daily lives, ethical decision-making has never been more critical. While AI can process vast amounts of data and identify patterns, it lacks the moral compass that guides human judgement. Navigating the ethical complexities of the digital age requires a nuanced understanding of both technological capabilities and human values.

Ethical decision-making involves considering the broader implications of our choices, especially when they impact others. In the context of AI, this includes addressing concerns about data privacy, algorithmic bias and the potential for unintended consequences. For instance, AI algorithms trained on biased data can perpetuate existing inequalities, leading to unfair outcomes in areas like hiring, lending or law enforcement. In lending, biased algorithms can quietly redraw the boundaries of economic opportunity. Credit-scoring systems trained on historical financial data may penalize applicants from certain neighbourhoods or employment backgrounds—not because they are higher risk, but because past exclusion has left thinner credit trails. What appears as neutral risk assessment can, in reality, harden structural inequality, making access to capital contingent on legacy rather than potential.

In law enforcement, the stakes are even higher. Predictive policing tools trained on historical crime data often concentrate surveillance in already over-policed communities, reinforcing cycles of suspicion and intervention. When past patterns of arrest become inputs for future deployment decisions, bias is not corrected—it is automated. Ethical decision-making, therefore, requires more than accuracy; it demands a conscious examination of whose history is being encoded, whose safety is prioritized and whose freedom may be compromised by statistical convenience.

To navigate these challenges, professionals must engage in continuous ethical reflection and dialogue. This involves questioning assumptions, seeking diverse perspectives and being transparent about decision-making processes. Establishing clear ethical guidelines and accountability mechanisms within organizations can help ensure that AI is developed and deployed responsibly.

Moreover, ethical decision-making requires balancing competing interests. For example, while AI can enhance efficiency and productivity, it may also lead to job displacement. Leaders must weigh the benefits of technological advancement against the potential social costs, striving to implement solutions that promote equity and inclusion. For example, when deploying AI-driven hiring or credit-scoring systems, a leader must ensure that efficiency gains do not come at the expense of marginalized groups being systematically excluded due to biased data or opaque decision rules.

Education and training in ethics are essential for professionals working with AI, not as abstract philosophy but as practical decision-making tools. Understanding frameworks like utilitarianism and deontology helps clarify *how* and *why* choices are made when trade-offs arise.

For instance, consider an AI system used by a city to optimize emergency response times. A utilitarian approach might prioritize routing ambulances to areas where the most lives can be statistically saved, while a deontological lens would question whether every neighbourhood is receiving equal moral consideration, regardless of numbers.

Similarly, in content moderation on social platforms, utilitarian logic may justify removing certain voices to reduce overall harm or misinformation, while deontological ethics would challenge whether silencing any group violates fundamental rights to expression. Ethical literacy allows professionals to recognize these tensions rather than hide behind "what the algorithm decided".

In practice, ethical training equips leaders to pause, ask better questions and design guardrails—ensuring AI systems don't merely optimize outcomes, but reflect the values societies choose to uphold.

Standing out in the AI era

In a world where AI can replicate many tasks, personal branding has become a vital tool for professionals seeking to differentiate themselves. Personal branding involves consciously shaping how others perceive you, highlighting your unique skills, values and experiences.

Artificial intelligence's ability to automate routine tasks means that human qualities like creativity, empathy and critical thinking are more valuable than ever. By showcasing these attributes through a strong personal brand, professionals can demonstrate their irreplaceable contributions to their fields.

Building a personal brand starts with self-awareness. Understanding your strengths, passions and values allows you to craft a narrative that authentically represents who you are. This narrative should be consistently communicated across various platforms, including social media, professional networks and personal websites. Staying up-to-date with AI advancements can set you apart from competitors and position you as an industry thought leader.

Content creation is a powerful way to establish thought leadership and share your expertise. Writing articles, giving talks or participating in podcasts enable you to contribute to industry conversations and build credibility. Engaging with your audience by responding to comments and participating in discussions further enhances your visibility and influence.

Social media is a vital tool for personal branding. Managing your social media presence can be a time-consuming and complex task. This is where AI can make a big difference. Artificial intelligence can help you analyze and track engagement metrics across multiple social media platforms, providing insights into what content is working and what isn't. By identifying the best times to post, AI can also help you optimize your social media posting schedule to increase engagement and reach.

Networking is another critical component of personal branding. Building relationships with peers, mentors and industry leaders can open doors to new opportunities and collaborations. Attending conferences, joining professional associations and participating in online communities help expand your reach and reinforce your brand.

In the AI era, it is also important to stay current with technological trends and continuously update your skills. Demonstrating adaptability and a commitment to lifelong learning signals to others that you are proactive and forward-thinking.

Ultimately, personal branding is about articulating your unique value proposition and making it visible to the world. By investing in your personal brand, you position yourself as a distinctive and indispensable professional in an increasingly automated landscape.

One of the central concerns is the risk of losing authenticity in a brand's messaging. Artificial intelligence algorithms can generate content that appears highly personalized and convincingly human, yet still lack the subtle voice, lived experience and intentionality that give a brand its distinctive character. Another concern lies in algorithmic bias: AI systems can amplify narrow perspectives, producing personalized recommendations that unintentionally exclude or misrepresent diverse audiences—ultimately damaging trust and alienating customers or stakeholders.

At the same time, when guided thoughtfully, AI can also strengthen authenticity rather than erode it by freeing human creators from repetitive tasks, enabling deeper audience insight, and allowing more time for deliberate storytelling, ethical oversight and creative refinement. The real risk, therefore, is not the presence of AI, but the absence of human judgement in how it is used.

The role of mentorship and community

I read an insightful quote the other day on the internet: "I asked AI how to get rich. It told me to 'invest in yourself.'"

Mentorship and community play pivotal roles in professional development, especially in an era characterized by rapid technological change. As AI reshapes industries, having access to guidance and support becomes increasingly important for navigating new challenges and opportunities.

Mentors provide valuable insights, share experiences and offer advice that can accelerate learning and career progression. They can help mentees identify their strengths, set goals and develop strategies for overcoming obstacles. The mentor-mentee relationship fosters personal growth and builds confidence, enabling individuals to take on new responsibilities and pursue ambitious objectives.

Communities, whether professional associations, online forums or informal networks, offer a sense of belonging and collective learning. Engaging with a community allows individuals to exchange ideas, stay informed about industry trends and collaborate on projects. These interactions can spark innovation, inspire creativity and provide a support system during times of change.

In the context of AI, mentorship and community engagement are crucial for staying abreast of technological advancements and understanding their implications. Mentors can guide mentees in acquiring new skills relevant to the evolving job market, while communities can facilitate knowledge sharing and collective problem-solving.

Organizations can foster mentorship and community by creating structured programs, encouraging cross-functional collaboration and promoting inclusive cultures. By investing in these social structures, companies not only support individual development but also enhance organizational resilience and adaptability.

Mentorship and community are essential components of a thriving professional ecosystem that provide the human connection and collective wisdom necessary to navigate the complexities of the AI-driven world.

Purpose—the heart of human motivation

When individuals understand how their work contributes to a larger mission, they are more likely to be committed and resilient even in the face of disruption. And unlike machines, which function on input-output logic, humans thrive on meaning. This is precisely where purpose becomes our most powerful differentiator in an AI-driven world.

Across professions from educators to engineers, healthcare workers to content creators those who are anchored in a sense of purpose demonstrate greater adaptability, higher creativity and deeper emotional intelligence. A teacher who believes they are shaping future citizens, or a nurse who views their job as healing lives—not just administering medication—will bring a level of commitment and humanity that no AI can replicate. Purpose fuels our drive to improve, connect and lead. It inspires us to stretch beyond job descriptions, ask difficult questions and find better ways forward.

In the workplace, organizations that clearly communicate a sense of collective purpose tend to attract more loyal, innovative and motivated employees. When companies align profit with purpose— when success is defined not just by shareholder returns but by the value delivered to society—employees feel like they are part of something bigger than themselves. And in a time when machines can crunch data faster and scale solutions wider than ever before, it is the human ability to act out of meaning that becomes the soul of progress.

But purpose is not always grand or world-changing. It can be quiet and personal. It may lie in nurturing a team, solving a persistent problem or creating art that moves people. What matters is that it is yours. Purpose is deeply personal and cannot be automated or outsourced. Artificial intelligence can optimize a task, but it cannot give our life direction. That is our job.

This means cultivating purpose must be intentional. Professionals need time and space for reflection on their values, their motivations and their goals. Journaling, mentoring, coaching and regular personal check-ins can help clarify what matters most. Communities, too, play a role here. Being around purpose-driven people helps reinforce and renew your own clarity of mission.

There is a deeper philosophical insight here too: in a world saturated with smart machines, what ultimately sets us apart is not just our intelligence but our intentionality. Machines can optimize, but only humans can aspire. Machines can learn, but only humans can long. Purpose is the flame that lights the path ahead by animating our reason, elevating our emotion and uniting our efforts. It is the final proof that we are, still and forever, human.

So if there is one enduring strategy to thrive in an age of AI, it is this: know your purpose. Live your purpose. Let it speak louder than your résumé, your metrics or your LinkedIn endorsements. Purpose isn't just a personal luxury; it is a professional necessity. Because in a world where machines can do so much, what makes you irreplaceable is knowing *why* you do it at all.

What do you think is AI's biggest enemy? Low battery.

How I learned it

By the early 2000s, I was the creative director of India's largest advertising agency. The titles were flattering, the rooms attentive, the work glamorous. Yet beneath the applause, something unsettled me. I sensed that in the advertising business identity itself was standing at the edge of a tectonic shift. The digital wave was rising. Automation was creeping into products and services. Software was standardizing what once required craft. Product life cycles were shrinking. Money was turning invisible. Speed was becoming virtue. And suddenly, excellence—real excellence—was no longer guaranteed to survive on reputation alone.

I asked myself a question that would quietly shape the next two and a half decades of my life: *What skills will still matter twenty years from now?*

Not the fashionable ones. Not the ones rewarded by the moment. The enduring ones. The answer I kept returning to was deceptively simple: strategic thinking.

At that time in India, "strategy" was narrowly defined—marketing strategy, media strategy and sometimes and brand strategy. I chose to expand it radically. Strategy became, for me, a way of seeing the world. I applied it to organizational growth, corporate responsibility, social communication, rural transformation, change management, visioning, policy influence and behavioural shifts. Strategy was not a function; it was a mindset. It was the ability to step back, see patterns, anticipate second and third-order effects and align actions with long-term meaning.

To pursue this seriously, I had to do something uncomfortable. I had to step down—internally—before the world pushed me down externally. I climbed off the ego-polished pedestal of creative leadership and sat back in the learner's humble asana. Once again, I became a student of life's *pathshaala*. I ordered books from Europe and the US. I joined discussion groups. I enrolled in short university courses. I read Edward de Bono obsessively. I studied and studied and studied—not to accumulate credentials, but to sharpen perspective.

Then, sometime around 2005 or 2006—just before the global financial crisis shook the world—I found what I had been unknowingly searching for all along. Two fields appeared before me like long-lost twins: behavioral science and behavioral economics.

Here were disciplines that finally explained why people behave the way they do—not the way textbooks assume they should. Pavlov. Watson. Kahneman. Tversky. Thaler. Suddenly, human irrationality was no longer a flaw to be corrected; it was a feature to be understood. Decision-making revealed itself as emotional, contextual, biased and beautifully messy. In that moment, I knew I had stumbled upon something profound. This was not a professional jackpot—it was an existential one.

India, at that time, barely spoke this language. So I looked outward—to professors in the US and Europe, to thinkers who had no reason to respond but did, to long conversations carried over fragile Skype connections in the years before YouTube became an algorithmic oracle. And then, almost organically, another door opened. Someone connected me with the social sector and the world of "strategy" overnight became a whole new thing to me. It suddenly became "change" from the "market growth" that I knew; it suddenly was "impact" from the "sales figures" we fought for every month end.

I widened my professional horizon beyond FMCG and mainstream marketing into the development and social impact space. I began working with nonprofits on meaningful communication, policy strategy and large-scale behaviour change. I was no longer selling products alone; I was helping ideas travel—ideas about health, dignity, the environment and equity—while still applying the rigour of brand thinking and strategic design. It was the same craft, but a different calling. And for the first time, everything I had learned began to converge into a purpose larger than myself.

When UNDP invited me to advise on their first global knowledge management initiative, I made a decision that surprised many. I left advertising. Entirely. I stepped into a world of global impact, public health, climate resilience and social transformation. It felt less like a career shift and more like a homecoming. Since 2006, I have worked across South Asia and Sub-Saharan Africa—helping governments design policies, helping communities reshape health behaviours and helping systems rediscover humanity. The accolades came later. What stayed was meaning.

Looking back now, through the lens of this book's final chapter, I see the pattern clearly. Every turning point in my life followed the same principle this chapter argues for: don't try to outrun the machine—outgrow the moment. Strategic thinking helped me see beyond immediate success. Emotional intelligence helped me work across cultures and power structures. Lifelong learning kept me relevant when industries collapsed. Ethics anchored my choices when efficiency tempted shortcuts. And purpose gave direction to everything else.

This chapter is not asking you to become extraordinary. It is asking you to become *intentional*. To choose growth over comfort. To choose values over velocity. To see AI not as a rival, but as a partner—one that amplifies what you bring to the table. Machines will learn faster. They will scale wider. They will imitate better. But they will not choose *why*. That remains our burden and our privilege.

If there is one lesson my journey has taught me, it is this: careers are not built by chasing trends, but by cultivating depth. Relevance does not come from knowing more than others, but from seeing more clearly than yesterday. And in an age of AI, the most radical act is not to become more efficient but to become more human.

We are not here to compete with code. We are here to write meaning into the systems we build. The future will belong not to those who adapt the fastest, but to those who align the deepest. And when the machines quietly and relentlessly ask us, *What should matter?*— may we have the courage, clarity and conscience to answer.

A COMPREHENSIVE TIMELINE OF ARTIFICIAL INTELLIGENCE (1950–2030)

1950s—The Foundational Decade

Year	Milestone	Significance
1950	Alan Turing publishes *Computing Machinery and Intelligence*; proposes the Turing Test	Establishes the philosophical basis of machine intelligence
1951	First neural network machine (SNARC) built by Marvin Minsky	Early attempt at machine learning
1956	Dartmouth Conference (McCarthy, Minsky, Rochester, Shannon)	Birth of artificial intelligence as a formal field
1957	Rosenblatt develops the Perceptron	Foundation of neural networks

1960s—Early Optimism

Year	Milestone	Significance
1961	First industrial robot introduced—Unimate	AI enters manufacturing
1964	ELIZA developed by Joseph Weizenbaum	First natural language processing chatbot

Year	Milestone	Significance
1969	Minsky & Papert publish *Perceptrons*	Reveals limits of early neural networks; AI winter begins

1970s—Expert Systems Emerge

Year	Milestone	Significance
1972	PROLOG programming language created	Becomes core to symbolic AI
1976	Knowledge-based systems gain	"Expert systems" era begins

1980s—AI Revival

Year	Milestone	Significance
1980	Digital Equipment Corporation deploys XCON	First major commercial expert system success
1986	Rumelhart, Hinton & Williams develop backpropagation	Revives neural networks; foundation of deep learning.

1990s—AI Goes Mainstream

Year	Milestone	Significance
1997	IBM's Deep Blue defeats chess champion Garry Kasparov	First major public triumph of AI over a world champion
1998–1999	Speech recognition and recommendation engines improve	AI begins shaping consumer tech.

2000s—Big Data + Better Algorithms

Year	Milestone	Significance
2002	Roomba launched	Autonomous robots enter homes
2006	Geoff Hinton coins the term deep learning	Neural networks return to global relevance
2009	Google launches self-driving car project	AI mobility revolution begins

2010s—Deep Learning Explosion

Year	Milestone	Significance
2011	IBM's Watson wins *Jeopardy!*	NLP (Natural Language Processing) surpasses human performance in specific tasks
2012	AlexNet wins ImageNet	Breakthrough in computer vision; deep learning takes over AI research
2014	Amazon Alexa + home assistants	AI begins reshaping domestic life
2016	AlphaGo beats Lee Sedol	Machine intuition surpasses human champions in complex strategy
2018	BERT created by Google	Major leap in contextual language understanding
2018	GPT-1 introduced by Open AI	First of OpenAI's large language models
2019	GPT-2 released	Text generation reaches near-human fluency

2020s—The Generative AI Era

Year	Milestone	Significance
2020	GPT-3 released	AI writes essays, code, poetry; multimodal abilities begin
2021	AlphaFold solves protein folding	AI transforms biological science
2022	DALL-E 2, Midjourney, Stable Diffusion	AI becomes a creative collaborator
2023	GPT-4 introduced	AI demonstrates advanced reasoning, multimodal analysis
2024	Surge of AI copilots in workplaces	AI transitions from tool to teammate
2025–2027 (Projected)	AI agents become autonomous task completers	Workflows begin to restructure around AI orchestration
2028–2030 (Projected)	AI is deeply embedded in governance, education, healthcare	Human–AI symbiosis becomes the norm; new ethical frameworks emerge

AI becomes:

- a co-worker

- a co-creator

- a personal analyst

- a civic infrastructure tool

- a behavioural mirror

- a societal force

The defining question shifts from *"What can AI do?"* to *"What do we choose to do with it?"*

Created by the author

SELECTED BIBLIOGRAPHY

Bostrom, N. (2014). *Superintelligence: Paths, Dangers, Strategies.* Oxford University Press.

Brown, T. (2009). *Change by Design: How Design Thinking Creates New Alternatives for Business And Society.* Harvard Business Press.

Crawford, K. (2021). *Atlas of AI: Power, Politics, and the Planetary Costs of Artificial Intelligence.* Yale University Press.

Christian, B. (2020). *The Alignment Problem: Machine Learning and Human Values.* W. W. Norton & Company.

Christensen, C. M. (1997). *The Innovator's Dilemma: When New Technologies Cause Great Firms to Fail.* Harvard Business Review Press.

Eubanks, V. (2018). *Automating Inequality: How High-Tech Tools Profile, Police, and Punish the Poor.* St. Martin's Press.

Harari, Y. N. (2016). *Homo Deus: A Brief History of Tomorrow.* Harper.

——.(2018). *21 Lessons for the 21st Century.* Spiegel & Grau.

——. (2024). *Nexus: Where Data, Power, and Humanity Collide*. Penguin Random House.

IDEO.org. (2015). *The Field Guide to Human-Centered Design*. IDEO.org.

Johnson, S. (2012). *Future Perfect: The Case for Progress in a Networked Age*. Riverhead Books.

Kahneman, D. (2011). *Thinking, Fast and Slow*. Farrar, Straus and Giroux.

Lanier, J. (2018). *Ten Arguments for Deleting Your Social Media Accounts Right Now*. Henry Holt and Co.

Liedtka, J., Salzman, R., and Azer, D. (2017). *Design Thinking for the Greater Good: Innovation in the Social Sector*. Columbia Business School Publishing.

Li, F.-F. (2020). TED Talk: How We're Teaching Computers to Understand Pictures. Retrieved from TED.com

Martin, R. (2009). *The Design of Business: Why Design Thinking is the Next Competitive Advantage*. Harvard Business Press.

Norman, D. A. (2013). *The Design of Everyday Things* (Revised and expanded edition). Basic Books.

O'Neil, C. (2016). *Weapons of Math Destruction: How Big Data Increases Inequality and Threatens Democracy*. Crown Publishing Group.

O'Reilly, T. (2017). *WTF?: What's the Future and Why It's Up To Us*. HarperBusiness.

Russell, S. (2019). *Human Compatible: Artificial Intelligence and the Problem of Control*. Viking.

Zuboff, S. (2019). *The Age of Surveillance Capitalism: The Fight for a Human Future at the New Frontier of Power*. PublicAffairs.

ACKNOWLEDGEMENTS

This book is the outcome of a long, winding conversation with ideas, people and with the times we live in. *Futureproof* did not emerge from a single discipline or moment of insight; it grew at the intersection of technology and humanity, strategy and ethics, design and doubt. I stand on the shoulders of thinkers, practitioners, institutions and communities who have shaped my questions long before I attempted to answer them in these pages.

My intellectual debt is deep and wide. The works of Nick Bostrom, Stuart Russell and Brian Christian sharpened my understanding of the promises and perils of advanced intelligence. Yuval Noah Harari's writings consistently challenged me to view technology not as destiny, but as a moral and civilizational choice. Shoshana Zuboff, Kate Crawford, Virginia Eubanks and Cathy O'Neil reminded me that power, bias and inequality are not side effects of technology, but often its design features. Daniel Kahneman's insights into human judgement, along with the foundations laid by behavioural economics, shaped how this book understands decision-making in an AI-saturated world.

Equally influential have been the thinkers and practitioners of design and systems change—Tim Brown, Roger Martin, Don Norman, Jeanne Liedtka and IDEO.org—who demonstrated that human-centred design is not a method, but a stance. Their work reinforced my belief that empathy, imagination and intentionality are not soft skills, but structural ones.

This book is also grounded in lived work. My research and strategy engagements across India, Sub-Saharan Africa and South Asia—documented through collaborations with Busara Center for Behavioural Economics, UNICEF, UNISDR, BBC Media Action and multiple government systems—have taught me what theory alone never could: that resilience is behavioural, trust is designed and change is always contextual. Communities in Bihar, Rajasthan, Bodoland Territorial Region, Assam, Ghana, Ethiopia, Kenya, Bangladesh, Afghanistan and the Maldives shaped this book as much as any library did.

I owe special gratitude to those who helped me grow, not just as a professional, but as a thinker navigating complexity. Prof. Ravi Dhar at Yale School of Management deepened my understanding of behavioural economics with rigour and generosity. Prof Sue Ellis at the BBC Academy expanded my writing, editorial and leadership lens. Dr Anand Pradhan and Prof. Gita Bamezai at the Indian Institute of Mass Communication grounded my thinking in research, public discourse and academic integrity. My journey at BBC Media Action was profoundly shaped by the leadership and trust of Priyanka Dutt and the creative vision of Radharani Mitra, both of whom helped me to have faith in the power of creative thinking and nudging. My heartfelt thanks to my respected teacher, Dipankar Sarkar, who from my childhood has relentlessly pushed me to aim higher, climb further and never settle for the comfortable peak.

My social research and strategic communication work with the Gates Foundation was deeply shaped and enriched by its country director Archna Vyas whose clarity of vision and intellectual generosity helped me understand how behavioural insight, when applied with purpose, can translate into meaningful and lasting global impact.

I am deeply grateful to Biswanath Dasgupta, editor-in-charge and creative director, *The Telegraph in Schools*, for graciously endorsing the book.

A special word of gratitude is owed to the editorial team at Om Books International, who transformed this manuscript into a book with immense care, rigour and belief. Working with them has been a deeply enriching experience. I am especially thankful to Jyotsna Mehta, my editor, for her patience, perseverance and grace in engaging with my stubborn attachment to voice, rhythm and narrative flow while still pushing the work to become sharper and clearer.

My sincere thanks to Editor-in-chief Shantanu Ray Chaudhuri who identified the spark in the manuscript early on and had the conviction to say "yes" to its intent and ambition.

And to Ajay Mago, the visionary publisher, whose instinctive understanding of what makes a winning book—both in substance and presence—ensured that this work receives the visibility and respect it deserves.

Finally, I acknowledge the invisible collaborators—students, practitioners, policymakers, program implementers, colleagues and readers—who continue to engage with me, challenge me and ask sharper, more critical questions. This book is for them. If *Futureproof* succeeds in anything at all, it is because it belongs to a shared inquiry: how to remain human, ethical and purposeful in an age of intelligent machines.